Preachers, Teachers

and Selected Short Features

More Explorations of

Jewish Life and Learning

Alberta Judaic Library

Calgary, 2019

Other books by Eliezer Segal:

Case Citation in the Babylonian Talmud: The Evidence of Tractate Neziqin, 1990.

The Babylonian Esther Midrash: A Critical Commentary, 3 volumes, 1993-1994.

Why Didn't I Learn This in Hebrew School, 1999.

Holidays, History and Halakhah, 2001.

Ask Now of the Days That Are Past, 2005.

From Sermon to Commentary: Expounding the Bible in Talmudic Babylonia, 2005.

In Those Days, at This Time: Holiness and History in the Jewish Calendar, 2007.

A Meeting-Place for the Wise: More Excursions into the Jewish Past and Present, 2008.

Sanctified Seasons, 2008.

Introducing Judaism, 2008.

Judaism—the eBook, 2008.

Reading Jewish Religious Texts, 2011.

For Signs and for Seasons, 2011.

On the Trails of Tradition: Explorations of Jewish Life and Learning, 2011.

The Most Precious Possession: The Ring of Polycrates in Ancient Religious Narratives, 2014.

A Time for Every Purpose, 2015.

Chronicles and Commentaries, 2015.

Beasts that Teach, Birds that Tell: Animal Language in Rabbinic and Classical Literatures, 2019.

Preachers, Teachers

and Selected Short Features

More Explorations of

Jewish Life and Learning

by

Eliezer Segal

Alberta Judaic Library

Calgary, 2019

© 2016-2019

16 – 310 Brookmere Rd SW

Calgary, Alberta, Canada

T2N 1N4

eliezer.segal@ucalgary.ca

http://www.ucalgary.ca/~elsegal

All illustrations are taken from Wikimedia or other sources in the public domain.

No part of this publication may be reproduced, stored in a retrieval system or transmitted, in any form or by any means, without the prior written consent of the author.

Table of Contents

The One that Got Away 1

Starting Off on the Right Foot 9

Who Built the Ark? Utnapishtim! 16

Flying out of a Rage 24

Symbolic Sarah 31

Go West, Young Jacob! 38

The Ultimate Space-Saver 45

Chariot of the God 52

Thrown to the Dogs 60

The Messiah Takes Manhattan 67

Ladies of Letters 74

Rabbis, Rationalists...and a Remedy that Roars 82

By the Time We Get to Phoenix 90

Moo-sical Mystics 99

Yellow is the New Red 107

Fetal Positions 115

That Was No Lady, That Was My Allegory 123

Saint Gamaliel 133

The Poem on the Pedestal	141
Arriving at Ararat	149
The Time of Our Life	157
A Preacher's Dream and an Artist's Vision	164
Cagney, Kelly...and a Coin Clattering in a Keg	172
Vital Organs	180
Wake-Up Call	187
What Will the Neighbours Think?	194
Testing the Waters	202
The Unkindness of Strangers	210
Speed Demon	218
It's My Party—and You'll Cry If I Want to	226
Dead Men Don't Sneeze	233
First Publication	239

The One that Got Away

The third-century Babylonian Jewish scholar known as Rabbah bar bar Ḥana used to travel back and forth between his native land and the land of Israel, serving as a conduit for the transmission of teachings of the foremost sages of the holy land to the Babylonian academies. Dozens of his teachings spanning a wide range of religious law fill the pages of the Talmud.

In spite of his respectable scholarly accomplishments, Rabbah is probably best known to posterity for a unique series of stories that were ascribed to him—and which the Talmud appended to a technical discussion about the laws for purchasing boats. In those tales Rabbah related fantastic sights and exploits that he experienced in the course of his travels to exotic places on land and sea. Some of those stories link to episodes from the Bible, while others have no obvious purpose other than (so it seems) to hold us spellbound by their astounding details.

Included among those tall tales is the following episode: "Once, as we were voyaging in a ship, we observed a certain fish. Its back was coated with sand out of which grass had sprouted. Assuming that it was dry land, we climbed up on its back, and set about baking and cooking. But when its back got hotter it turned over—and had our ship not been lying nearby, we would have drowned."

Whatever we might think about the veracity of the rabbi's report, we should note that similar legends about sailors who were confounded by island-sized fish were in wide circulation in the ancient world, among the Greeks and the Romans as well as in Iranian myths that could have been familiar to Jews in Babylonia. The pioneering Latin naturalist Pliny the Elder collected numerous reports—of varying degrees of scientific credibility—about giant sea creatures and monsters such as the "Physeter" and the "Pistris" that made a powerful impression on the imaginations of his readers. The satirist Lucian of Samosata, in a parody of the genre of fanciful travel memoirs, included an episode in which the narrator's ship was swallowed up by a sea-creature so immense that its insides were populated by a thriving urban community.

A very similar tale was included in a Christian work known as the "*Physiologus*." Scholarly opinions about the date of its original Greek text range from the second to the fourth centuries, after which it enjoyed immense popularity in translations to Latin, Ethiopic and numerous other languages. It took its name (which was apparently not its original title) from the fictitious premise that it was a scientific lexicon based on the teachings of a learned naturalist. The work is in reality a fanciful bestiary of mythical and actual creatures; it identifies traits of those creatures that lend themselves to moral or allegorical expositions.

The passage from the *Physiologus* that concerns us provides far more extensive detail than the Talmud's terse story, as it describes a sea monster that is known in Greek as the "aspidochelone" [meaning: "asp-turtle"]. This beast is a giant whale and its skin has the appearance of a sandy beach like that on a seashore. For that reason, when it swims with its back floating above the surface of the water, sailors mistake it for an island and are enticed into parking their vessels and venturing ashore to enjoy a respite from their sea voyages. Convinced that they are on *terra firma*, they affix wooden pegs on which to moor their ships, and then go about lighting fires to cook their meals.

St. Brendan and the fish Jasconius: Woodcut from the medieval English work "The Journey of St. Brendan"

One of the most popular versions of this legend appears in

the Arabic *Thousand and One Nights*, in the first of the seven voyages of the intrepid seafarer Sinbad. As Sinbad tells it, his crew had sailed seven days on their journey from Basra in Iraq, when they espied a small, sunlit island that was as fair as the garden of Eden, adorned with lush vegetation. Securing his vessel at a safe distance from the island, Sinbad ventured by himself in a flimsy dingy to pick some herbs which he planned to blend into a luscious recipe (also containing hashish). While he was occupied with that task, he heard an alarmed yell from the mother ship alerting him that he was in imminent peril and must return forthwith to the craft, since what lay beneath his feet was not an island but a gigantic fish. At that very moment the creature leapt up making terrifying noises. Our hero tried to escape in his frail dingy, but it was quickly blown out of the waters. Unlike Rabbah bar bar Ḥana, the crew of Sinbad's ship did not hasten to his rescue, but fled in panic, leaving him to swim off to harrowingly dangerous and thrilling new adventures.

Now some of us might be perfectly satisfied to enjoy such captivating yarns enhanced by spectacular special effects. For the most part, however, students of the Talmud approached Rabba bar bar Ḥana's adventures from a more austere religious perspective, and insisted that they must contain some edifying message. Some commentators, like Rabbi Yom Tov ben Abraham Ishbili (Ritva), strove to justify them on the grounds that, outlandish though they might appear, the reports are based on actual wonders of the natural world, so that they serve to enhance our appreciation of the all-powerful creator who fashioned them all. Alternatively, the fearsome beasts might also originate in inspired dreams that were intended to teach us profound truths.

The great homilist Rabbi Ephraim Solomon Luntshits offered an allegorical explanation of the episode: the ship represents the human soul destined to navigate the stormy seas of life. The person who strives to be perfectly righteous must take special care to avoid associating with the wicked—who are symbolized in the tale by the alluring (but thorny) foliage on the "island." At first it is friendly and accommodating, but after it has succeeded in garnering your trust, it reverts to its true character and tries to attack and destroy you. In this way, the sinister sea monster fooled Rabbah bar bar Ḥana and his companions into thinking it was a secure, lifeless tract of dry land—but then it heated up and pounced on them. Were it not for the divine assistance that is vouchsafed to us (represented metaphorically as the boat waiting nearby ready to come to the rescue), all of us mortals would be defenseless victims of the evil powers.

Indeed, Rabbi Luntshits' approach is in line with Christian readings of the Aspidochelon passage in the *Physiologus*. That beast was understood to symbolize the deceptions of the devil who causes unwary mortals to be enticed by hunger, thirst and sinful desires until they are drawn to eternal torment.

Other classic commentators, including Ritva and Rabbi Samuel Edels (Maharsha), interpreted the story not as a lesson about the moral fate of the individual, but as a paradigm for Jewish national survival. Thus, the deceptively hospitable island exemplifies the situation of the Jews in Persia and Media at the time of the Purim story—and one presumes, the feelings of some of the commentators' contemporaries. Those Jews were convinced that they had been comfortably assimilated into their current environments and exempted from the curses normally associated with Jewish life in the diaspora. However, they would soon be reminded that they were still subject to the bitter perils of exile. Salvation could only be achieved through repentance and by acknowledging that the ultimate redemption had not yet arrived.

And I suppose that this is surprisingly apt advice for us all to heed, as humans and as Jews. We should take care to prepare ourselves for the eventuality that the calm surfaces on which we are treading might suddenly plunge into the depths and leave us thrashing.

But of course, such mishaps only happen in fanciful legends from bygone ages.

Bibliography:

Bacher, Wilhelm. *Die Agada der babylonischen Amoräer: ein Beitrag zur Geschichte der Agada und zur Einleitung in den babylonischen Talmud.* Hildesheim: G. Olms, 1967.

Epstein-Halevi, Elimelech. *Agadot Ha-Amora'im*. Tel-Aviv: Dvir, 1977.
Grunebaum, Gustave E. von. *Medieval Islam: A Study in Cultural Orientation*. Chicago: University of Chicago Press, 2005.
Hole, Richard. *Remarks on the Arabian Nights Entertainments: In Which the Origin of Sinbad's Voyages, and Other Oriental Fictions, Is Particularly Considered*. London: T. Cadell, Junior and W. Davies, 1797.
Kiperwasser, Reuven. "Rabba Bar Bar Channa's Voyages." *Jerusalem Studies in Hebrew Literature* 22 (2008-2007): 215–42. [Hebrew]
Kiperwasser, Reuven, and Shapira, Dan D. Y. "Irano-Talmuidica II: Leviathan, Behemoth and the 'Domestication' of Iranian Mythological Creatures in Eschatological Narratives of the Babylonian Talmud." In *Shoshannat Yaakov: Jewish and Iranian Studies in Honor of Yaakov Elman*, edited by Shai Secunda and Steven Fine, 203–35. The Brill Reference Library of Judaism. Brill, 2012.
Montgomery, J. E. "Al-Sindibad and Polyphemus: Reflections on the Genesis of an Archetype." In *Myths, Historical Archetypes, and Symbolic Figures in Arabic Literature: Towards a New Hermeneutic Approach: Proceedings of the International Symposium in Beirut, June 25th - June 30th, 1996*, edited by Angelika Neuwirth, 437–466. Beiruter Texte und Studien 64. Beirut: In Kommission bei Franz Steiner Verlag Stuttgart, 1999.
Patai, Raphael. "Jewish Seafaring in Ancient Times." *Jewish Quarterly Review* 32, no. 1 (1941): 1–26.
Silverstein, Alan. "From Markets to Marvels: Jews on the Maritime Route to China ca. 850-ca. 950 CE." *Journal of Jewish Studies* 58, no. 1 (Spr 2007): 91–104.

Slifkin, Nosson. "Sacred Monsters: Mysterious and Mythical Creatures of Scripture, Talmud and Midrash." Brooklyn, N.Y: Zoo Torah, 2007.

Stemberger, G. "Münchhausen und die Apokalyptik." *Journal for the Study of Judaism* 20, no. 1 (1989.

Williams, Wes. *Monsters and Their Meanings in Early Modern Culture: Mighty Magic*. Oxford: Oxford University Press, 2011.

Yassif, Eli. *The Hebrew Folktale: History, Genre, Meaning*. Translated by Jacqueline S. Teitelbaum. Folklore Studies in Translation. Bloomington: Indiana University Press, 1999.

Starting Off on the Right Foot

That arch-heretic Baruch Spinoza did not believe that authentic religion has any legitimate business enacting laws for societies or individuals. He was consequently dismissive of the minute regulations that are so central to the law of Moses and to traditional Jewish life. In his "Theological Political Treatise" he argued that the Torah's laws do not really express the lessons of divine reason, but were intended to serve the more pragmatic objective of allowing Moses to govern an unruly people who did not yet have the political maturity to obey laws or authority because of their inherent moral value. The Torah therefore instilled in the Hebrews a mentality that bound them to the law through every single trivial action of their lives. "They were not allowed to plough, to sow, to reap, nor even to eat, to clothe themselves, to shave, to rejoice, or in fact to do anything whatever as they liked, but were bound to follow the directions given in the law." Whatever justification such a regimen might have had in the days of Moses, Spinoza insisted that it has no validity in a modern enlightened society where the Jews do not govern their own political state.

Judaism's allegedly obsessive tendency to micromanage our behaviour is often epitomized in the cliché that the halakhah even dictates the proper sequence for putting on and lacing our shoes. And indeed, unlike many such stereotypes about traditional Judaism, this one happens to be quite true. The Shulḥan 'Arukh instructs, as part of one's morning routine:

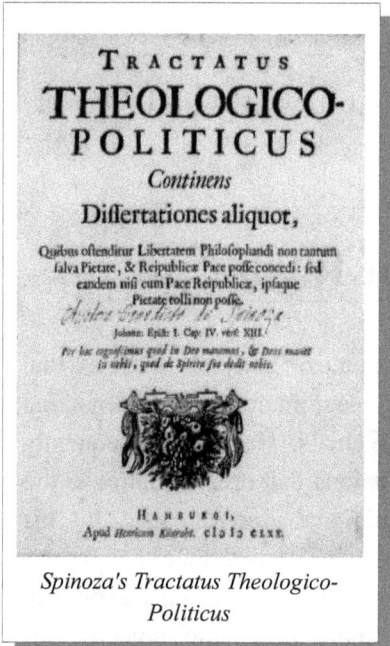

Spinoza's Tractatus Theologico-Politicus

"One should put on the right shoe first but not tie it yet; then put on the left shoe and tie it; then proceed to tie the right one."

This ruling is based on a discussion in the Babylonian Talmud. The passage in question cites an assortment of different opinions as to the correct sequence—though nobody challenges the basic premise that the mode of putting on footwear falls within the legitimate scope of religious law. The Talmud text opens with a quotation from Rabbi Yoḥanan that the left shoe should take precedence, a rule that he derives from the case of tefillin where the normal practice (at least for right-handed persons) is to bind them to the left arm, based on a midrashic interpretation of the relevant scriptural text. However, Rabbi Yoḥanan's position is juxtaposed to a teaching from an earlier tradition, that one should put on the right shoe before the left, which would be consistent with the usual tendency of Jewish law to favour the right side.

The Babylonian scholars in the Talmud disagreed about how to deal with this contradiction when formulating normative practice. Rav Joseph argued that since the matter was in dispute among respected authorities, either practice is acceptable and it makes no difference whether one begins with the right or left shoe. Similarly, Rav Ashi reported that his teacher Rav Kahana was not particular about the order.

Rav Joseph's student Abayé was not happy with his teacher's indecisive approach: after all, we do not really know how Rabbi Yoḥanan would have responded to the contradictory tradition cited in the Talmud. Normally, an earlier source overrides a later one, and there is reason to suppose that if he had been aware of the older tradition, he would have retracted his own ruling accordingly. On the other hand, maybe he did know of it, and yet he knowingly upheld his original view nonetheless; and perhaps his position was also founded on an earlier tradition that he had heard! If the earlier sages insisted so strongly on maintaining their respective positions, is it proper for us to treat them as if they were optional, or matters of subjective preference?

The Jerusalem Talmud preserved a different version of Rabbi Yoḥanan's teaching. It states there that when his attendant Simeon bar Ba, a Babylonian immigrant, handed him his right sandal first in accordance with what he thought was the proper etiquette, the master chided him: "Babylonian, don't act this way, since that is not how the early authorities used to conduct themselves. Rather, one should first put on the left shoe and afterwards the right." He goes on to explain that It is only an injured limb that normally gets shod first, and it is therefore considered "disrespectful" to a healthy right foot when we treat it as if it were infirm.

In the Babylonian Talmud, a solution to the dilemma of the contrary rulings was provided by Rav Nahman bar Isaac who described the personal custom of the "God-fearing" Mar son of Rabina, who would satisfy both opinions by putting on the right shoe first, but then tying the left lace first.

Rabbi Isaac ben Asher in the Tosafot commentary noted that it is indeed more appropriate that tying the laces should be the act that begins on the left, in that it was derived from the case of the tefillin where the essence of the precept consists of tying or binding.

The laissez-faire attitude favoured by Rav Joseph and Rav Kahana in the Talmud was evidently accepted by most of the early medieval codifiers of Jewish religious law, since the topic is skipped over entirely in the compilations of Rabbi Isaac Alfasi, Maimonides and others.

The omission of the rule from early law codes is likely the reason why it attracted surprisingly little attention from among proponents of the Kabbalah. Normally, any topic that emphasizes the importance of left and right was ideal grist for the interpretative mills of the medieval kabbalists who asserted that spatial right and left correspond to the divine attributes of mercy and justice that define the metaphysical harmony of the universe, and which humans can influence by means of the correct performance of the commandments.

Nonetheless, in the early fourteenth century Rabbi Jacob ben Asher's *Arba'ah Ṭurim* ruled in accordance with Mar son of Rabina's custom: right shoe first, left lace first. A few generations later, an important kabbalistic compendium known as the *Sefer Ha-Ḳanah*, probably composed by a Byzantine author toward the end of the fourteenth century, devised an elaborate metaphor to show how paying careful attention to the respective sides of justice and mercy when donning footwear constitutes an effective symbolic preparation for appeasing the gatekeepers who control our access to the throne of the merciful supreme King.

In the late sixteenth century, the ruling of the *Arba'ah Ṭurim* was incorporated into Rabbi Joseph Caro's authoritative Shulḥan 'Arukh, thereby establishing it as the normative practice for subsequent generations.

With all due deference to Spinoza, punctilious observance of the rules governing the correct wearing and lacing of shoes was not confined to the blindly obedient or the starry-eyed kabbalists. Several scholars with decidedly rationalist inclinations found something of great value in these rules—if not for their own sake, then as instances of the Jewish genius for instilling religious meaning into all the diverse areas of human activity.

For example, Rabbi Menaḥem Meiri of Perpignan, Provence, who excelled at applying standards of clarity and logical precision to the elucidation of the Talmud, pointed out how this simple practice exemplifies the highest ideals of Torah living:

> All the actions of Torah scholars are directed toward a single goal. Even when they are occupied with their material needs, their hearts are directed toward the worship of the Lord. You are aware that when putting on shoes, one recites the blessing "[Blessed is God] who has provided me with all my needs"... Similarly, when putting on shoes, we should put on the right one first in order to remind ourselves that in all matters it is preferable to keep "on the right side" and to honour one who walks in the right path.

Bibliography:

Halbertal, Moshe. *Between Torah and Wisdom: Rabbi Menachem Ha-Meiri and the Maimonidean Halakhists in Provence.* Jerusalem: Magnes Press, 2000. [Hebrew]

Halivni, David. *Sources and Traditions: A Source Critical Commentary on the Talmud. Vol. Tractate Shabbath*. Jerusalem: The Jewish Theological Seminary of America, 1982. [Hebrew]

Krauss, Samuel. *Talmudische Archäologie*. Vol. 1. 3 vols. Schriften von Gesellschaft zur fürderrung der wissenschaft des Judentums. Grundriss der gesamtswissenschaft des Judentums. Leipzig: G. Fock, 1910.

Kushnir-Oron, M. *The Sefer Ha-Peli'ah and the Sefer Ha-Kanah*. Pirsume Ha-Midrasha Le-Limmudim Mitqadmim. Jerusalem: Hebrew University Faculty of Arts, 1980. [Hebrew]

Pely, Hagai. "The Book of 'Kanah' and The Book of 'Peliah': Literal and Esoteric Meaning of the Halakhah." *Tarbiz* 77, no. 2 (2008): 271–93. [Hebrew]

———. "The Ways of 'Adjudication' in 'Sefer Ha-Kanah' and 'Sefer Ha-Peliah.'" *Daat: A Journal of Jewish Philosophy & Kabbalah* 68-69 (2010): 187–224. [Hebrew]

Who Built the Ark? Utnapishtim!

It is not surprising that adherents of old-time religion have often been extremely suspicious of the study of biblical literature and history by secular scholars. Most notably, by subjecting the text to literary and historical analysis, those scholars argued that the "law of Moses" is in reality a patchwork of several separate documents that were composed over centuries and embody diverse attitudes and world-views.

And even Jews who might otherwise have been receptive to aspects of the "documentary hypothesis" had good reason to be disturbed by the persuasively argued thesis of the nineteenth-century German philologist Julius Wellhausen who used the theory to support his claim that the noble moral vision of the Israelite prophets degenerated during and after the Babylonian exile into a spiritless cult dominated by a priestly caste and obsessed with the mechanical observance of rituals.

In the wake of this problematic relationship between faith and secular scholarship, it was natural to expect Jews to feel hostility, or at least indifference, to the exciting discoveries in Near Eastern archeology that were taking place in the nineteenth and early twentieth centuries, as freshly unearthed artifacts began to shed their light on the cultures of the nations that bordered on biblical Israel. Similar suspicions typified the attitudes of Christians as they found that their literal belief in the factual accuracy of their scriptures was being compromised by the evidence of the ancient stones, and especially by the texts preserved in newly deciphered cuneiform scripts.

An extraordinary case occurred in 1853 with the discovery of a set of clay tablets from the seventh century B.C.E. from the library of the Assyrian capital Nineveh, containing a saga known as the "Epic of Gilgamesh." This text recounted the adventures of the wise king Gilgamesh, of godly lineage. The popular Mesopotamian epic drew upon Sumerian prototypes, and translations and adaptations have been found in many ancient lands. Among the numerous details that invited comparisons with the Hebrew book of Genesis, the most conspicuous was its tale, recounted in the eleventh tablet, of a flood that the gods unleashed in order to destroy all humanity—with the sole exception of Gilgamesh's ancestor Utnapishtim who was instructed to build a boat to rescue himself, his household, selected companions and some animals. In the end, Mr. and Mrs. Utnapishtim were rewarded with the gift of immortality. It was the quest for that cherished secret that impelled Gilgamesh to seek him out and listen to his tale.

The first public announcement about the Epic of Gilgamesh was presented before the Society of Biblical Archaeology in 1872 in London by a scholar named George Smith, and it instantly caught the imaginations of readers throughout Europe.

The discovery was also found worthy of mention in the pioneering Hebrew weekly *"Ha-Maggid"* that appeared in Lyck, Prussia and was dedicated to keeping its readership informed about the most important and relevant developments in international news. The journal's editors generally steered a moderate course between modern enlightenment and traditional Judaism. They ignored any scholarly developments that called into question the divine origin of the Torah; however they did take a lively interest in assorted archaeological finds in Israel, Egypt and Mesopotamia; and in almost every volume they included reports about them for the edification of their eastern European Jewish audience.

Tablet of the Epic of Gilgamesh from Nineveh, now in the British Museum

The report in *Ha-Maggid* proclaimed enthusiastically, "It is understandable that this announcement has made a very powerful impression, because it provides us with a very ancient attestation for what is written in the holy Torah—and it will stifle the mouths of those who deny its truth." Instances such as this, it was thought, could help vindicate the demand for scientific education and worldly knowledge among Jews who were wary of secular culture.

Banner of the Ha-Maggid newspaper

However, it was not obvious to everybody that the Epic of Gilgamesh and the kindred literary texts that continued to appear over the coming decades necessarily provided support for traditional Judaism. Whereas pious believers might feel reassured by the fact that pagan writers were adding their testimony to the Torah's tale of a global flood, more skeptical minds were interpreting the evidence in precisely the opposite direction: All we can say is that myths about a flood were in wide circulation among the ancient Babylonians and Sumerians, and the Hebrews were merely copying those legends from the dominant civilizations—the geographical details of the biblical story indicate its Mesopotamian provenance—adapting them slightly and incorporating them into their sacred scriptures. Viewed from the perspective of what came to be known in German as the "Bibel und Babel" school, is Israelite literature really any different from any of the other myth-loving civilizations of the age?

More recent scholarship has tended to take a more balanced approach to assessing the flood stories as they appear on Hebrew parchment and on cuneiform tablets. Although we may appreciate how the first modern readers of the Gilgamesh epic were excited primarily by its uncanny similarities to the stories in the Bible, deeper reflexion eventually resulted in an increased awareness of glaring differences between their respective world-views. Clearly, the biblical author has extensively reworked the Mesopotamian materials to express Israelite values that stand in powerful opposition to the pagan ethos.

In the pagan versions, our world is perceived as the outcome of conflicts between squabbling deities who represent diverse powers of nature and often cause collateral damage in the earthly realm. This is reflected in the background to the flood: most of the gods, led by the hostile Enlil, are determined to unleash it without giving advanced warning to any of the humans. The god Ea, however, breaks rank and alerts Utnapishtim in a dream that he should get to work constructing a boat. Afterwards, the gods themselves are alarmed by the destructive power that they have unleashed and they begin to argue about the assigning of blame for the debacle.

The Hebrew God, by contrast, is in complete control of the events, and there is no dissident supernatural power for him to contend with. Indeed, the Genesis narratives are marked by the unprecedented absence of mythical themes, a unique phenomenon among the cultures of that age.

Most significantly—unlike the biblical story in which humanity brought the disaster on themselves because of their moral perversity, the flood legend in the old Babylonian and Assyrian fragments seems to imply a motive that sounds utterly trivial: "In those days the world teemed, the people multiplied, the world bellowed like a wild bull, and the great god was aroused by the clamour. Enlil heard the clamour and he said to the gods in council, 'The uproar of mankind is intolerable and sleep is no longer possible on account of the din.'" What it seems to be saying is that the human race must be eliminated because their racket is interfering with the gods' sleep!

In Genesis Noah was chosen to be saved because he was deemed righteous, whereas no real explanation is given for Ea's decision to rescue Utnapishtim and his companions, and this detail was of no evident concern to the authors of the Mesopotamian legend. And yet precisely that question is the crucial one in the Hebrew tradition for which righteousness and wickedness are the main criteria for judging mortals.

For modern readers, these kinds of observations are far more meaningful than simplistic questions about the factual accuracy of the creation or flood narratives. They speak to core moral qualities that lie at the heart of any proper appreciation of the Torah's struggle against paganism, and Judaism's lasting impact on civilization.

Bibliography:

Dundes, Alan, ed. The Flood Myth. Berkeley and Los Angeles: University of California Press, 1988.

Fishbane, Michael. Biblical Myth and Rabbinic Mythmaking. Oxford and New York: Oxford University Press, 2003.

Cassuto, Umberto. A Commentary on the Book of Genesis, Part 1: From Adam to Noah. Publications of the Perry Foundation for Biblical Research in the Hebrew University of Jerusalem. Jerusalem: Magnes Press, 1961.

Heidel, Alexander. The Gilgamesh Epic and Old Testament Parallels. Chicago: University of Chicago Press, 1963.

Kaufmann, Yehezkel. "The Bible and Mythological Polytheism." Journal of Biblical Literature 70, no. 3 (September 1951): 179–97.

———. The Religion of Israel, from Its Beginnings to the Babylonian Exile. Translated by Moshe Greenberg. University of Chicago Press, 1960.

Kramer, Samuel Noah. History Begins at Sumer: Thirty-Nine Firsts in Man's Recorded History. 3rd rev. ed. Philadelphia: University of Pennsylvania Press, 1981.

Salmon, Yosef. "David Gordon and 'Ha-Maggid': Changing Attitudes toward Jewish Nationalism, 1860-1882." Modern Judaism 17, no. 2 (1997): 109–24.

———. "David Gordon and the Periodical Ha-maggid / 1860—1882." Zion 47, no. 2 (1982): 145–64.

Sarna, Nahum M. Understanding Genesis. [1st ed.]. Heritage of Biblical Israel, v. 1. New York: Jewish Theological Seminary of America, 1966.

Shavit, Yaacov. "'Truth Shall Spring out of the Earth': The Development of Jewish Popular Interest in Archaeology in

Eretz-Israel." *Cathedra for the History of Eretz Israel and its Yishuv* 44 (1987): 27–54.

Flying out of a Rage

The good old traditional curse does not get much respect in our culture.

Now, those curses spoken by God in the Bible make some sense; for the most part, they contain threats of punishments that will be inflicted on the disobedient and the wrongdoers by a deity who is capable of following through with his threats. But, human curses are quite a different matter. It popular parlance they tend to be equated with simple insults, or even obscenities. The more precise meaning of a curse—that a person's words can wield the supernatural power to inflict harm on victim—is not taken very seriously in our sophisticated scientific intellectual climate.

Although the malevolent potential of a curse is something that is regarded with serious trepidation in Jewish folklore, among Kabbalists and other more credulous types, Jewish thinkers who studied philosophy and subscribed to more rational interpretations of the tradition were less sympathetic to the notion that humanly uttered curses have the ability to hurt their targets.

Initially it would appear that their skepticism is contradicted by the words of scripture: After all, if there is no substance to a curse, then why does the Torah include prohibitions against them among the commandments.

In his Arabic treatise on the 613 commandments, Moses Maimonides devoted an extensive and insightful excursus to this question. His starting point was the verse in Leviticus: "thou shalt not curse the deaf," from which the Jewish oral tradition derived a comprehensive prohibition against cursing one's fellow. What, then, was the point of singling out the deaf for special attention in this text?

Page from a Yemenite manuscript of Maimonides' Book of Commandments

Maimonides concluded from this anomaly that the opposition to cursing cannot possibly be because of any harm that it can cause to its victim. After all, deaf people will not even be aware of the curses or insults that have been directed against them. Indeed, he concludes that this is precisely the lesson that we are intended to deduce. The Torah's purpose in forbidding curses was not rooted in the shame or insult to which the victim has been subjected; if that were the case, then there would be no sin in cursing the deaf, seeing as they do not normally suffer distress from a curse—and yet the Torah admonishes us that such cursing is nonetheless forbidden! This must be because the Torah is not approaching the matter from the perspective of the victim, but rather it is concerned principally with the psychological and moral effects on the person who is *doing the cursing*.

By way of explanation, Maimonides provides a fascinating mental typology of people who allow themselves to indulge in enraged indignation. When such persons have suffered a wrong, they are roused to an anger that will not abate until the wrongdoer (real or imagined) has been made to suffer harm to a degree that is proportional to the damage he has inflicted.

Whatever the real measure of guilt or harm that has been perpetrated (and it is not clear that such matters can be objectively measured), every victim makes their own mental assessment of the seriousness of the offense against them, and hence of the appropriate degree of retaliation that can provide satisfaction for the wrong. At the lowest tier are those serene souls who can be calmed by some token ranting or vocal curses against the offenders. This outlet will be most satisfying when offenders are not deaf, and can actually hear the nasty things that are being said about them. As we progress along the scale of vengeance, some wrongs will warrant destruction of property, bodily injury causing pain or disfigurement—and in the most extreme cases, the wronged party will not feel that justice has been achieved with anything less than taking the life of the offender.

Thus, Maimonides seems to be assuming that the harshness of the vengeance derives less from the gravity of the offense than from the personality of the avenger. But the intelligent religious personality must not allow itself to be swayed by irrational emotions like rage and vengefulness. Most significantly, if we tolerate or encourage the most innocuous level of venting rage—through cursing or other forms of verbal abuse—then we are effectively opening the floodgates to uncontrollable torrents of violent reprisals and feuding. It was for this reason that the Torah had the foresight to insist that we preempt this destructive pattern before it gets out of hand, by prohibiting the least harmful manifestation of vengeful anger: the harmless cursing of those who do not even realize that they have been cursed.

Maimonides' point was aptly summarized by Rabbi Bahya bar Asher: "And all this is stated in order to encourage people to be careful about what they say, and not to adopt bad habits. The prohibition is not grounded in the effect it has on the fellow who hears the curse, but on the subsequent behaviour of the curser. If a person can be prudent in this matter with respect to the deaf, it goes without saying that one will act with restraint in the treatment of those who are capable of hearing."

Not all the Jewish commentators, even among those who took a rational approach to the tradition, shared Maimonides' certainty that curses cannot really harm their targets. The thirteenth-century author of the popular compendium *Sefer Ha-Ḥinnukh* on the commandments of the Torah resigned himself to the acknowledgment that our limited human intelligence is incapable of grasping the true nature of curses and how they might affect their victims. It is an indisputable empirical fact that most people in the world take curses seriously.

Furthermore, Jewish tradition shared the philosophers' assertion that our ability to speak is the most sublime human faculty, the unique ability that elevates us above all other creatures. It is therefore not unreasonable to posit that this divine gift, identified as the divine breath of life that was breathed into man, is imbued with the power to influence others for good or for evil.

Even if the curse's impact is not of a metaphysical or magical nature, *Sefer Ha-Ḥinnukh* allows that the psychological damage is quite real. Viewed in this way, the Torah may outlaw curses as a form of violent assault. Although the mental anguish caused by a curse might be rooted entirely in the victim's delusions about its efficacy, it still constitutes a kind of injury. Hence, by discouraging individuals from freely exchanging curses, insults and other forms of verbal abuse, Jewish law is lowering the collective level of volatility, and thereby helping to promote social harmony.

In his attempt to devise a rational basis for curses, *Sefer*

Ḥa-Ḥinnukh invokes a principle of Maimonidean philosophy, that those elevated souls who have refined their spirits through metaphysical contemplation can achieve remarkable results through the words that they speak. He argues that the Torah's ban on curses is founded on the premise that this verbal power is real. The author appreciates that this approach is at odds with that of Maimonides who utterly denied the reality of curses.

Each of these approaches has had its supporters among Jewish thinkers. I would like to imagine that if they were to be thrown into a room together, then the disagreements over similar questions of theology, exegesis or religious law would be discussed respectfully, even amicably. Unfortunately, I have too much experience with academic feuding to be completely confident about the prospects.

Nevertheless, I shall try to refrain from uttering curses (even under my breath) against those who violate the norms of civil debate.

Bibliography:

Silverberg, David. "'You Shall Not Curse a Deaf Man.'" pdf. *Maimonides Heritage Center*, 2005. https://www.mhcny.org/parasha/1030.pdf.

Slifkin, Natan. "A Curse Upon Thee!" Blog. *Rationalist Judaism*, 2010. http://www.rationalistjudaism.com/2010/05/curse-upon-thee.html.

Tabory, Binyamin. "Parashat Balak: Kelala (Cursing)." Text. *The Weekly Mitzva: Yeshivat Har Etzion*, 2013. http://etzion.org.il/en/kelala-cursing.

Trachtenberg, Joshua. *Jewish Magic and Superstition: A Study in Folk Religion*. Temple Books. New York: Atheneum, 1982.

Symbolic Sarah

When Alexander the Great established the city of Alexandria in Egypt, to which he proudly attached his own name, he intended it to serve as a showcase for the finest achievements of Greek culture and the conduit through which real civilization (which of course was an exclusively Greek monopoly) could be brought to the unenlightened denizens of the orient.

The Jewish community that developed there assimilated many aspects of the Greek ethos, but for the most part remained loyal to their own religious traditions. This produced a fascinating scholarly synthesis as they learned to blend philosophical rationalism with the study of the Torah.

Most of what we know about the Alexandrian Jewish endeavour in biblical interpretation has reached us in the oeuvre of the first-century C.E. scholar known as Philo

Judaeus. His detailed analyses of passages from the Torah offer precious glimpses into the variety and complexity of the exegetical approaches; and he often compares his own readings with those of his contemporaries who were involved in similar projects.

Probably the most distinctive innovation of the Alexandrian Jewish exegetes was their application of the allegorical method to the sacred text. That is to say, they would explain that certain events or personalities in the Bible should be understood as symbols representing concepts or values. This method, which Greek scholars had applied to the works of Homer, had an inherently subversive aspect to it; if used to excess, it could lead to the denial of the literal truth of the Bible, or (as would later become a major point of contention between traditional Judaism and nascent Christianity) to the abandonment of the commandments after one had grasped their allegorical meanings. Philo himself tried to steer a moderate course in this matter. He criticized the more extreme allegorists who had ceased observing the traditional religious rituals. He seemed to prefer applying the allegorical method only in cases where the literal sense raised interpretative or philosophical difficulties.

We see some remarkable examples of the Alexandrian allegorical approach in Philo's depictions of the matriarch Sarah.

Fragment from Greek manuscript of Philo's "Allegories of the Sacred Laws" © *Bodleian Library, University of Oxford*

In several of his commentaries Philo equates Sarah with the noblest kind of philosophical or theological wisdom. Thus, in a discourse about Sarah's dismissal of her Egyptian maid Hagar, he contrasts the mistress Sarah with Hagar who is made to symbolize inferior secular culture. Only philosophical learning qualifies for the honour and reverence due to a true "wife" (Sarah) while lesser studies are merely her "handmaidens" (Hagar). As such, after they have served their purpose it is essential to graduate to a higher plane—to send away Hagar—and not remain at the elementary level. In this case, it is likely that Philo's chose to interpret this episode allegorically because of the moral difficulties raised by its literal plot in such troubling matters as Abraham's supplanting his wife with a surrogate, and Sarah's cruel treatment of Hagar.

When commenting on God's promise to Abraham that Sarah will bear him an heir—"and I will bless her, and give thee a son from her"—Philo cites no fewer than four different attempts to explain the (ostensibly superfluous) words "from her," which in the Greek translation (which served as the basis for those commentaries) can have the sense of "outside of her." Allegorically understanding that Sarah symbolizes the soul in its quest for spiritual perfection, the interpreters explained (in various ways) that the Torah is teaching us how true spiritual wisdom cannot be generated by the individual, but it must be receptive to benevolence from "outside"—from God who generously bestows this wisdom upon us.

Alternatively, in her allegorical guise as the personification of Virtue, Sarah was being depicted as the mother of all good things, where their father is God. Here as well, Philo indicates that he was impelled to interpret the biblical text in an allegorical manner because he felt that the literal meaning—that a woman who was explicitly described as "barren" was able to conceive a child—ran contrary to reason. On the other hand, if we choose to understand that the Torah is not speaking about the historical Sarah but about a symbol of the human soul, which is "barren" as long as it is pursuing wicked thoughts but becomes fruitful when it fortifies itself against the temptations of the flesh, then the story becomes morally edifying.

In fact, it seems that Philo had problems coming to terms with Abraham and Sarah's stable marriage. According to the Greek philosophical values with which he identified, true philosophers ought to relinquish the pleasures of the flesh and devote themselves entirely to metaphysical contemplation. Women represent erotic temptation, and as such their company should be avoided other than whatever is necessary to produce a family. In keeping with this manner of thinking, Philo explains the Torah's statement that "it ceased to be with Sarah after the manner of women" as if it were saying that, as the embodiment of spiritual virtue, she elected to become celibate and voluntarily withdrew from domestic life with her husband. As such, she was now qualified to devote herself to a spiritual "marriage" with God which generated spiritual offspring.

Elsewhere, Philo cites still another allegorical interpretation to that text which he ascribes to certain "natural scientists," and with which he felt obliged to disagree. They chose to understand that Abraham, the husband, was meant to symbolize the Mind, while Sarah represents Virtue This imagery was suggested by her name which means "princess"—and of course in the spiritual realm nothing governs more powerfully than Virtue. Those scientific interpreters were aware that on the literal, physical plane, women are invariably passive parties who are subordinate to their husbands and receive everything from them. This Greek ideal is not quite in keeping with the active role that is assigned to Sarah in the Torah's narrative, or with the philosophical doctrine that the Mind is subject to the dictates of Virtue in its pursuit of spiritual perfection. Therefore they found it convenient to construe Abraham and Sarah as allegorical concepts that are outside the norms of human family dynamics. True, in a family setting wives should be dominated by their husbands; but in the world of philosophical concepts Virtue is an active force that exerts a decisive influence on the Mind by bestowing sound moral counsel.

Philo was sympathetic to the basic premise of the scientists' argument, but was too much of a male chauvinist to countenance a reversal of the gender roles even at an abstract theoretical level. He therefore chose a different solution to the conundrum, by turning the allegory around (arguing that previous interpreters had been misled by the grammatical genders of the operative Greek words). In reality, Philo argued, Abraham symbolized the active power of Virtue, while Sarah was the passive Mind—accurately reflecting the ideal gender hierarchy of a family.

And so—-will the real Sarah please stand up!

Are you Wisdom, the Soul, Virtue, or Mind?

Although there is no doubt much to be learned from allegorical interpretations of the Torah, I personally prefer to be inspired by our mother Sarah as a complex and very real flesh-and-blood human being.

Bibliography:

Amir, Yehoshua. "The Transference of Greek Allegories to Biblical Motifs in Philo." In *Nourished with Peace: Studies in*

Hellenistic Judaism in Memory of Samuel Sandmel, edited by Edward Greenspahn, Earl Hilgert, and Burton Lee Mack, 15–25. Chico, CA: Scholars Press, 1984.

Barrett, C. K. "The Allegory of Abraham, Sarah, and Hagar in the Argument of Galatians." In *Rechtfertigung: Festschrift Für Ernst Käsemann Zum 70. Geburtstag*, edited by J. Friedrich, W. Pöhlmann, and P. Stuhlmacher, 1–16. Tübingen: Mohr Siebeck, 1976.

Belkin, Samuel. *The Midrash of Philo*. Edited by Elazar Hurvitz. New York: Yeshiva University Press, 1989. [Hebrew]

Borgen, Peder. *Philo of Alexandria: An Exegete for His Time*. Supplements to Novum Testamentum. Leiden: Brill, 1997.

Niehoff, Maren R. "Mother and Maiden, Sister and Spouse: Sarah in Philonic Midrash." *Harvard Theological Review* 97, no. 4 (2004): 413–44.

Sly, Dorothy. *Philo's Perception of Women*. Brown Judaic Studies 209. Atlanta: Scholars Press, 1990.

Stein, Edmund. *Die allegorische exegese des Philo aus Alexandreia*. Beihefte zur Zeitschrift für die alttestamentliche Wissenschaft 51. Giessen: A. Töpelmann, 1929.

Wegner, Judith Romney. "Philo's Portrayal of Women: Hebraic or Hellenic?" In *"Women Like This": New Perspectives on Jewish Women in the Greco-Roman World*, edited by Amy-Jill Levine, 41–66. Society of Biblical LIterature: Early Judaism and Its Literature 1. Atlanta: Scholars Press, 1991.

Wolfson, Harry Austryn. *Philo: Foundations of Religious Philosophy in Judaism, Christianity, and Islam*. Cambridge MA: Harvard University Press, 1948.

Go West, Young Jacob!

Stephen Vincent Benét is a name that is not heard much these days, though some of his short stories still show up in standard anthologies of American Literature. The Pulitzer Prize winning author came from an established American military family that had no apparent Jewish connections. Nevertheless, his interest in portraying and interpreting the American experience include at least one story with a decidedly Jewish theme. "Jacob and the Indians" was first published in the May 14 1938 issue of the *Saturday Evening Post*, and in the following year was included in Benét's collection *Tales before Midnight*.

The plot concerns the adventures of Jacob Stein, a bookish young Jew from Europe who was making a meagre living as a peddler in Philadelphia. The struggle of the uncouth Ashkenazic newcomers to be accepted by their cultured Sephardic coreligionists is a recurring motif. Determined to earn some more money and impress a young lady, young Jacob ventures out into the wilds of western Pennsylvania to involve himself in the fur trade in dangerously exciting Indian country. The encounter of the naïve talmudic scholar with the wild west is reminiscent of the exploits of Avram Belinski (Gene Wilder's character) in "the Frisco Kid." When Jacob returns to the city, he is a rugged frontiersman, and he has become so fascinated with the limitless possibilities of the American west that he is not particularly perturbed to find out that his former "rose of Sharon" for whom he originally undertook his quest has meanwhile been married to another.

Apart from Benét's general evocation of American society at that time, he clearly did some research into the dynamics of the Jewish community. The sentence structure sometimes reflects foreign rhythms that sound like Yiddish ("To Philadelphia he came") and the prose is sprinkled with Hebrew and Yiddish expressions, such as "chedar" (not a cheese but an elementary school), "the preacher Koheleth," "Schnorrer," impatience expressed by "nu," and even a female demon named Iggereth-beth-Mathlan—slightly garbled from the talmudic "Agrat bat Maḥlat." On the other hand, he also inserts some made-up phrases that are intended to sound like Hebrew adages; such as "protection of the strong is like a rock and a well," or "who lies down in the straw with a dog gets up with fleas" (the latter was probably coined by Benjamin Franklin).

 It is likely that the Jacob the hero was based on a certain Jacob I. Cohen (1744-1823), a Bavarian-born fur trader and friend of Daniel Boone who became a leading figure in the Philadelphia Jewish community. Benét's Jacob Stein was born in the town of Rettelsheim, Germany; as far as I can tell this is a fictitious locality, though Germany would fit the migration patterns of the time. Various speech patterns, customs and idioms that are embedded in the story seem more appropriate to Yiddish-speakers from Poland or Russia.

Another historical personage whom Benét incorporated into his character was Abraham Chapman, a Canadian trader who was captured by Indians in Detroit. As he was being burned at the stake, he asked for something to drink, but the soup that he was given was so scalding that he angrily hurled it at his captors. Such behaviour was unheard of among the Indians, and they presumed that the man was insane; which according to their laws earned him an exemption from execution.

Benét tells a virtually identical story about Jacob Stein in Pennsylvania. Notwithstanding its factual historical basis, like much of Benét's prose it also evokes biblical associations, notably with the tale of David who feigned madness to save his life from Achish king of Gat when fleeing from King Saul.

Indeed, it is in his skillful use of biblical motifs that I find Benét most fascinating. For example, Jacob Stein had a rival for the heart of his boss's lovely daughter Miriam Ettelson: Meyer Kappelhuist was a robust Dutch-born Indian trader with a red face and red hairs on the backs of his hands. It was in order to outdo Meyer's wealth and attractiveness to women that Jacob set out on his westward journey.

Of course for readers of the Bible, Meyer Kappelhuist immediately brings up associations with Jacob's twin brother Esau, the red-haired, hirsute hunter whose ambivalent relationship with Jacob drove the latter into exile both for personal safety and to find himself a wife.

The comparison is most evident in Benét's description of Jacob Stein's return to civilization. One of the first people he meets is Meyer Kappelhuist. They greet each other civilly, but as in the midrashic accounts that ascribed malicious motives to Esau, Jacob Stein "did not like the look in the red-haired man's eyes." When Meyer suggests that they continue their travels together, Jacob cautiously declines the invitation and decides to take a different route, even as the biblical Jacob did with Esau. In Benét's tale it turned out that Meyer Kappelhuist was scalped and killed by Indians, and Jacob accepted the duty of burying his remains.

The biblical language that most pervades the story of Jacob and the Indians is that which relates to the land itself: Jacob declares his plan to "go forth into the wilderness," and throughout the story the vast and limitless American frontier is designated by expressions like "wilderness," "the land of Canaan," "a view across the Jordan" or "Promised Land."

Jacob's mentor Raphael Sanchez (who seems to act as the author's voice in the narrative) speaks poignantly of his motives for immigrating to the New World: "It was for the promise—the promise of [William] Penn—that this land should be an habitation and a refuge, not only for the Gentiles." The Jews will have an equal share in the destiny of this unique new land, a share which must be earned.

Truly, Benét projected back onto the heroes of his story a vision of America that was messianic. He contrasted it with the rapacious European imperialist powers who seized possession of their colonial territories only to control and exploit their economic riches. America, by contrast, is a land that is cultivated by the hard work of its own residents. "One pays for the land of Canaan; one pays in blood and sweat." The redemption that lay in the American frontier would benefit not only Jacob's descendants, but "nations yet to come."

Indeed, although the young scholar Jacob had received a traditional Jewish education that was vividly steeped in the scriptural imagery of Jerusalem perched atop the Temple mount, Benét describes how that "white city set on a hill" came to be transformed in Jacob's heart into "a great and open landscape, ready for nations."

Those of us who remain devoted to the physical city of Jerusalem and to the strengthening of a Jewish homeland on our historic territory will doubtless feel uneasy at the American writer's co-opting of our deeply held national and religious convictions—though I am certain that they accurately reflect the attitudes of many Jews and Christians in the times of Jacob Stein and of Stephen Vincent Benét.

Nevertheless, the ideals which they expressed with such articulate passion—of redemption that must be earned through hard labour, and of a nationalism that seeks to share its bounty with all humanity—should still resonate with us, whether on the North American frontier or in our middle-eastern promised land.

Bibliography:

Baron, Joseph L., ed. *Candles in the Night: Jewish Tales by Gentile Authors*. New York: Farrar & Rinehart, 1940.

Godfrey, Sheldon J., and Judy Godfrey. *Search Out the Land: The Jews and the Growth of Equality in British Colonial America, 1740-1867*. Montreal & Kingston, London, Buffalo: McGill-Queen's University Press, 1995.

Marcus, Jacob Rader. *The Jew in the American World: A Source Book*. Wayne State University Press, 1996.

Reisner, Neil. "Philadelphia." In *The Jewish Traveler: Hadassah Magazine's Guide to the World's Jewish Communities and Sights*, edited by Alan M. Tigay, 400–404. Northvale, NJ: Jason Aronson, 1994.

Sarna, Jonathan D. "Jacob. I. Cohen." *Dictionary of Virginia Biography*. Richmond: Library of Virginia, 2006.

———. "Jacob I. Cohen and the 350th Anniversary of American Jewish Life." *Beth Ahabah Museum and Archives Generations* 2 (May 2005): 1, 3, 8, 12, 14.

Shea, Laura. In *Stephen Vincent Benet: Essays on His Life and Work*, edited by David Garrett Izzo and Lincoln Konkle, 92–127. Jefferson, NC: McFarland, 2002.

Vogel, Dan. "Stephen Vincent Benét and the Jews of Philadelphia: A Lesson in Colonial History." *Studies in American Jewish Literature (1981-)* 20 (2001): 62–68.

The Ultimate Space-Saver

Modern technology has devised many ingenious ways to make more efficient use of space and to miniaturize objects so that they perform their functions without leaving large footprints. Nonetheless, to the best of my knowledge, we have not yet reached the stage where we can produce structures that literally occupy no space at all.

It would appear that Jewish lore ascribed such impressive qualities to architectural masterpieces of the past, especially to the holy Temple of Jerusalem.

Take for example the passage in the Mishnah *Avot* that relates the experiences of the throngs of pilgrims who assembled for the major festivals. "They would be constricted when standing, but had adequate space to prostrate themselves." Rashi explained that this was a truly miraculous occurrence—a twofold miracle, in fact. Not only would the

Detail from relief, Auch Cathedral, France: the Ark of the Covenant with cherubs

bodies of the worshippers be elevated above the ground to prevent their intruding on each other's individual space, but the area would actually expand to separate them, in order to insure privacy when they were reciting their personal confessions.

However, not all the commentators were willing to interpret the passage in blatantly supernatural terms. Rabbi Menahem Meiri wrote more prosaically that the worshippers were forced to stand on their tiptoes to keep from trampling on their neighbours' toes. According to Maimonides, the Mishnah was merely describing the subjective feelings of the worshippers who became oblivious to the crowding because they were overwhelmed by feelings of intense reverence for the holy place.

In other talmudic passages, the rabbis read various biblical texts as implying that hundreds of thousands of Israelites were squeezed together in the doorway or courtyard of the Tabernacle for the dedication ceremonies; or atop the small rock that produced water for the congregation in the wilderness.

In a similar vein, the talmudic sages claimed regarding Solomon's Temple, that "the ark was not included in the measurement" of the twenty cubits of the sanctuary's length. The simple sense of this statement is probably that the area contained by the ark was not included in the calculation of the ten cubits separating each of its sides from the wall of the inner sanctuary. However, in the Babylonian Talmud the statement was construed as proof that the ark "was standing miraculously." Rashi explained this to mean that the ark "did not occupy any space at all that would diminish from the dimensions of the space of the room"!

Rashi's interpretation follows logically from the analogy that the Talmud drew between the case of the ark and a similar phenomenon involving the dimensions of the cherubs and their wings. The third-century sage Samuel calculated that it is impossible to fit the two cherubs into the twenty cubits of the sanctuary's length, since the length of each of their wings was five cubits; so if they were allowed to spread to their full capacity, the four wings would span twenty cubits, and would not leave any room for the parts of cherubs' bodies that were not coextensive with the wings. This led Samuel to the conclusion that the cherubs and their wings did not occupy any measurable physical space in the sanctuary. The fact that the Talmud equated the cases of the ark and of the cherubs demonstrates that, in their opinion, the essence of the miracle lay in the premise that neither object occupied any space in the sanctuary.

Galen

The miracles in question were evidently characterized by violations of the laws of geometry: if we were to measure from either edge of the ark until the Sanctuary wall, we would come up with a distance of ten full cubits, even though the ark itself was two and a half cubits wide and the total length of the Sanctuary was exactly twenty cubits.

In most of the Greek and Roman philosophical schools that were contemporary with the talmudic rabbis, it was widely assumed that even God is subject to the fundamental laws of logic and mathematics. On these grounds, several philosophers ridiculed religious beliefs that defied basic logic, such as the doctrine that the universe was created out of nothing.

The famed physician and philosopher Galen (129 – c. 200) chided the Torah for believing that there are no limits to what God can do. "We however do not hold this; we say that certain things are inherently impossible and that God does not even attempt such things at all."

In the twelfth century, the Jewish physician Maimonides was aware of Galen's position and of his accusations about the Torah's irrationality. Maimonides refuted those charges, insisting that they were based on a misrepresentation of Jewish teachings. "Moses' real opinion is that the power to do impossible things cannot be ascribed to God." While there may be room for legitimate philosophical debate over which things are inherently impossible (such as the doctrine of creation out of nothing), this does not alter the basic axiom that even God acts within the principles of rationality, which include the laws of mathematics.

It would appear that the traditions that spoke literally of the ark or cherubs not occupying any space in the sanctuary would have been treated by Maimonides as no different from a claim that two and two equal five. People who believe in miracles of this sort are not enhancing the Almighty's greatness—quite the contrary, this kind of primitive credulity is characteristic of "those who are ignorant of mathematics and ...know only the words in isolation but do not comprehend their true meanings."

In the end, Maimonides determined that the tradition about pilgrims standing crowded but bowing spaciously, if taken literally, misrepresented the capabilities of the omnipotent deity, notwithstanding the whimsical embellishments of the rabbis.

In spite of Maimonides' defense of Judaism's intellectual sophistication, a survey of rabbinic texts would seem to bear out some of the allegations that were directed by Galen and others against the uncritical Jewish acceptance of impossible miracles. The sages of the Talmud and the Midrash remained largely unaffected by the philosophical views that were prevalent in their Greek-thinking environment. This strikes us as all the more astonishing when we bear in mind that, at about the same time, the question of God's power to violate logical rules was the topic of vehement debates between the philosophers and the representatives of revealed religious traditions, and that the uncritical Jewish belief in miracles had provided ammunition for assaults on the intellectual cogency of Judaism (and of Christianity).

Come to think of it, in our brave new world of quantum mechanics, wormholes, non-Euclidian geometry and nanotechnology, the notion of zero-space objects need no longer be dismissed as absurdly illogical. Indeed, it might offer renewed hope for us commuters who have to squeeze ourselves into packed trains or overloaded urban parking lots.

Bibliography:

Dienstag, Jacob Israel. "Introduction: The Relationship of Maimonides to His Non-Jewish Predecessors; an Alphabetical Survey." In *Studies in Maimonides and St. Thomas Aquinas*, xxxvii – xxxix. Bibliotheca Maimonidica 1. New York: Ktav, 1975.

Goldin, Judah. "A Philosophical Session in a Tannaite Academy." In *Essays in Greco-Roman and Related Talmudic Literature*, 366–86. New York: Ktav, 1977.

Guttmann, Julius. *The Philosophy of Judaism: The History of Jewish Philosophy from Biblical Times to Franz Rosenzweig*. Northvale, NJ: J. Aronson, 1988.

Harvey, Warren Zev. "Rabbinic Attitudes Toward Philosophy." In *"Open Thou Mine Eyes ...": Essays on Aggadah and Judaica Presented to Rabbi William G Braude on His Eightieth Birthday and Dedicated to His Memory*, 83–101. Hoboken, NJ: Ktav, 1992.

Husik, Isaac. *A History of Mediaeval Jewish Philosophy*. Mineola, NY: Dover Publications, 2002.

Rabinovitch, N. L. "The Concept of Possibility in Maimonides." *Tarbiz* 44, no. 1 (1975): 159–71.

Rokeah, David. *Jews, Pagans and Christians in Conflict*. Leiden and Jerusalem: E J Brill and Magnes Press, 1982.

Schacht, J., and Max Meyerrhof. "Maimonides against Galen, on Philosophy and Cosmogeny." *Bulletin of the Faculty of Arts of the University of Cairo* 5, no. 1 (1937): 53–88.

Segal, Eliezer. "'The Few Contained the Many': Rabbinic Perspectives on the Miraculous and the Impossible." *Journal of Jewish Studies* 54, no. 2 (2003): 273–82.

Stern, Menahem. *Greek and Latin Authors on Jews and Judaism*. Fontes Ad Res Judaicas Spectantes. Jerusalem: Israel Academy of Sciences and Humanities, 1974.

Walzer, Richard. *Galen on Jews and Christians [microform*. Oxford Classical and Philosophical Monographs. London: Oxford University Press, 1949.

Chariot of the God

When archaeologists first began to excavate ancient synagogues in Israel from the Byzantine era, the discoveries of elaborate mosaics on their floors came as an unsettling surprise to many people. Especially puzzling was the recurrence of one particular motif: a wheel consisting of the twelve zodiac signs, at the centre of which stood a mythological representation of the sun portrayed—according to the Greek convention—as the deity Helios driving a four-horse chariot.

Modern Jews had long since accepted the rationalist verdict of Maimonides that astrology is a silly superstition that is adamantly opposed by "authentic" Judaism. And of course, the graphic portrayal of a heathen god in a site devoted to monotheistic worship seemed altogether incomprehensible.

Indeed, some scholars have continued to interpret all this as evidence that the average Jews who worshipped on those mosaic floors observed an eclectic blend of Hebrew monotheism and Hellenistic spirituality; but they had little interest in the austere legalism of the rabbis who (it was argued) constituted no more than a tiny and isolated sect removed from the Jewish masses. Others argued that those mosaics expressed an ancient priestly ideology, which was preoccupied with the sun and advocated a liturgical division into twenty-four divisions, corresponding to the ancient Sadducee calendar.

Zodiac floors have been found or attested in about half a dozen sites scattered through the land of Israel, including Hammat

The Zodiac mosaic floor from Beit Alpha

Tiberias, Beit Alpha, Na'aran, Susiya, Husifa, and Sepphoris. They conform to a very standardized structure: in the centre sits the hub containing the sun-chariot, around which extends the wheel whose twelve spokes or slices are identified by the

Hebrew names and symbols of the constellations, and sometimes by the names of the months. Because the rooms and their floors are square, this design leaves room for four triangular corners that are devoted to the four seasons—identified, as per the standard talmudic convention, by the names of their first months: Tishrei, Ṭevet, Nisan and Tammuz. This too is a bit odd, given that the middle eastern climate does not really have four seasons, but merely a rainy and a dry time. However, the solstices and equinoxes are objective meteorological facts—and after all, those four corners had to be filled with something. It has been suggested that the zodiac motif was originally and primarily used on domed ceilings, but ceilings do not survive the ravages of history, so it is only the synagogue floors that remain.

Comparative studies reveal that similar motifs were quite widespread in architecture throughout the Mediterranean basin in the pre-Byzantine world, though the pagan versions were considerably more diverse than their Jewish counterparts. The christianization of the empire in the fourth century inspired an aggressive ideological opposition to all manifestations of astrology; and at least one church spokesman wrote derisively of the Jewish tendency to perpetuate pagan folly. Indeed, some scholars count this among the numerous instances where Jews adopted a foreign practice and continued to uphold it tenaciously long after the gentiles themselves had abandoned it.

Scholarship has had several decades to ponder the anomalies of the zodiac mosaics, but no real consensus has emerged. The old notion that rabbinic Judaism is inherently opposed to graphic art has long since been abandoned. It is also quite obvious that many Jews did acknowledge some type of astrology, though this outlook may have been more prominent in Babylonia, the birthplace of that ancient science, than in the land of Israel.

The scholarly questions have shifted, for the most part, from: how were the zodiac floors possible? to: why were they so prevalent? and: how did they fit in with Jewish values and synagogue practice? The answers that have been proposed are too manifold to survey here, and I shall confine myself to a few theories that make sense to me.

One can hardly overstate the importance of the calendar to Jewish life, with its intricate sequence of annual dates set aside for the commemoration of historical exploits and tragedies, as well as marking the cycles of nature and agriculture. Much of this sequence is celebrated through communal worship, scriptural readings and preaching in the synagogues.

In spite of their centrality to the religious rhythms, the Hebrew months offer relatively little symbolic potential of the sort that would be of use to homilists or poets. In the Torah they are given no names at all, but are merely identified by number. Eventually, the Jews adopted their Babylonian names, but those names are usually obscure Akkadian words, or (as in the case of Tammuz) actual pagan gods. By equating the months with their astrological signs, the worshippers could associate them with familiar inoffensive themes, such as rams, scales, water-vessels and the like, that could be easily incorporated into sermons and liturgical poetry. We observe this practice in several poetic texts by classic liturgical poets, such as Eleazar Kallir and Yannai, in which themes such as the blessings of water and rain or the devastation of Jerusalem are illustrated by references to the zodiac signs.

It also seems probable that for Jews who lived after the twilight of Greek and Roman paganism, a personification of the sun riding a chariot no longer conjured up associations with the mighty Helios or Sol Invictus. In the case of the Sepphoris mosaic, it is possible that the artists intentionally refrained from motifs that overtly evoked the sun god. At any rate, the primitive portrayals in the Byzantine mosaics have a crude cartoon-like quality to them. By then the image had become a religiously neutral one for representing the sun, in a manner analogous to our own casual invoking of Norse or Roman deities in the English names of our months and weekdays. And after all, the image of "chariots of God" is found in the Bible. It is in fact arguable that the consistent linking of the sun to a wheeled chariot is a distinctly Jewish development that has no precise equivalent in pagan art. Some rabbinic interpretations identified the human-like figure enthroned atop the mysterious chariot in Ezekiel's famous vision as Metatron, the "prince of the divine countenance," the foremost angel who bore the name of his Master and played a prominent role in ancient Jewish mysticism.

An early medieval midrash deftly illustrates how the figure of the sun at the reins of a divine chariot would enhance liturgical allusions to the sacred seasons. *Pirḳé de-Rabbi*

Eliezer, expounding references from Ecclesiastes and Psalms, depicted the chariot emblazoned with the letters of the divine name and led by angels, dramatically running its course through the heavens, switching direction at each of the four seasons, 'as it says (Psalm 19:6), 'it is like a hero, eager to run his course.'"

From my own perspective in the midst of the frigid Canadian winter, it is tempting to imagine that some worshippers might have found in their synagogues' mosaic decorations a reassurance that the sun was hastening toward them on its swift solar-driven vehicle to bring tidings of a warm summer ahead.

Bibliography:

Englard, Yaffa. "Mosaics as Midrash: The Zodiacs of the Ancient Synagogues and the Conflict Between Judaism and Christianity." *Review of Rabbinic Judaism* 6, no. 2–3 (2003): 189–214.

Fine, Steven. *Art and Judaism in the Greco-Roman World: Toward a New Jewish Archaeology.* Cambridge: Cambridge University Press, 2005.

———. "Art and the Liturgical Context of the Sepphoris Synagogue Mosaic." In *Galilee: Confluence of Cultures: Proceedings of the Second International Conference on the Galilee, January 1997*, edited by Eric M. Meyers, 227–237. Winona Lake IN: Eisenbrauns, 1999.

Foerster, Gideon. "The Zodiac in Ancient Synagogues and Its Place in Jewish Thought." *Eretz Israel* 19 (1988): 225–54. [Hebrew]

Goodenough, Erwin Ramsdell. *Jewish Symbols in the Greco-Roman Period.* New York: Pantheon, 1953.

Hachlili, Rachel. *Ancient Synagogues—Archaeology and Art: New Discoveries and Current Research.* Brill, 2013.

———. "Zodiac in Ancient Jewish Art: Representation and Significance." *Bulletin of the American Schools of Oriental Research,* no. 228 (1977): 61–77.

Mack, Hananel. "The Unique Character of the Zippori Synagogue Mosaic and Eretz Israel Midrashim." *Cathedra* 88 (1998): 39–56. [Hebrew]

Magness, Jodi. "Heaven on Earth: Helios and the Zodiac Cycle in Ancient Palestinian Synagogues." *Dumbarton Oaks Papers* 59 (2005): 1–52.

Miller, Stuart S. "'Epigraphical' Rabbis, Helios, and Psalm 19: Were the Synagogues of Archaeology and the Synagogues of the Sages One and the Same?" *Jewish Quarterly Review* 94, no. 1 (2004): 27–76.

Roussin, Lucille A. "The Zodiac in Synagogue Decoration." In *Archaeology and the Galilee: Texts and Contexts in the Graeco-Roman and Byzantine Periods,* edited by Douglas Ray Edwards and C. Thomas McCollough, 83–96. South Florida Studies in the History of Judaism 143. Atlanta: Scholars Press, 1997.

Sonne, Isaiah. "The Zodiac Theme in Ancient Synagogues and in Hebrew Printed Books." *Studies in Bibliography and Booklore* 1, no. 1 (1954): 3–13.

Weiss, Zeev. "The Zodiac in Ancient Synagogue Art: Cyclical Order and Divine Power." In *La Mosaïque Gréco-Romaine. IX,* edited by Hélène Morlier, 1119–30. Collection de l'École Française de Rome 352. Rome: École française de Rome, 2005.

Weiss, Zeev, and Ehud Netzer. "The Sepphoris Synagogue: Deciphering an Ancient Message Through Its Archaeological and Socio-Historical Contexts." Jerusalem: Israel Exploration Society, 2005.

Yahalom, Joseph. *Poetry and Society in Jewish Galilee of Late Antiquity.* Sifriyat "Helal ben Hayim." Tel-Aviv: Hakibbutz Hameuchad and Yad Izhak Ben-Zvi, 1999. [Hebrew]

———. "The Sepphoris Synagogue Mosaic and Its Story." In *From Dura to Sepphoris; Studies in Jewish Art and Society in Late Antiquity*, edited by Lee I. Levine and Zeev Weiss, 83–91. Portsmouth RI: Journal of Roman Archaeology, 2000.

Thrown to the Dogs

It is well known that the biblical dietary laws prohibit the consumption of meat that has not been slaughtered according to the required procedures. In this connection, the Torah commands: "neither shall ye eat any flesh that is torn of beasts in the field." So what may we do if we find ourselves in possession of such non-kosher meat? The text continues: "ye shall cast it to the dogs."

Now, some readers might naively suppose that the expression "cast it to the dogs" is simply an idiomatic way of stating that the carrion is unfit for any human consumption and therefore has to be discarded. However, talmudic law inferred from this verse that it is permissible to derive benefit from non-kosher meat. Moreover, the Jewish commentators, convinced that every word in the Torah was chosen with perfect care and precision, were spurred to ask why dogs were singled out for mention as the beneficiaries of the disqualified meat rather than, say, cats.

From the perspective of the ancient rabbis, the principles of divine justice demanded that the canines must have done something worthy to merit this preferred treatment. They found such an instance in the last of the Egyptian plagues, when Moses reassured the Israelites that absolute security would prevail in their homes while the Egyptians were enduring the horrible deaths of their firstborn. The expression employed by the Torah is: "but against any of the children of Israel shall not a dog move his tongue." A midrashic tradition explained that the dogs, though they barked continually to hound the Egyptian oppressors while they were burying their dead, maintained a respectful silence for the Israelites. It was this simple act of pious restraint that earned the ancient dogs and their progeny a God-given right to discarded non-kosher meat.

Rabbi Meir Abulafia referred to that tradition in order to explain a statement in the Talmud that "the dog recognizes its master, but the cat does not recognize its master." Rabbi Meir understood that the "master" being referred to was none other than the Master of the Universe, and that the canine species were endowed with a religious sensibility that found expression in their obedient behaviour during the Egyptian exodus.

Most of the commentators were not as willing as Rabbi Abulafia to ascribe spiritual virtues to simple mutts. They argued more prosaically that the "master" that the Talmud had in mind was the animal's human owner. Rabbi

Jacob Ibn Habib observed "This is the way of the world, that a dog recognizes a master and follows him wherever he goes in order to protect him. However, this is not so with cats."

The nineteenth-century exegete Rabbi Henokh Zundel of Bialostok, in his *Etz Yosef* commentary to the Midrash, was puzzled why Rabbi Abulafia had proposed such a seemingly unlikely interpretation of the talmudic passage. He suggested that it was rooted in his personal observations that cats too are, after all, domesticated creatures who acknowledge their owners and remain attached to the homes of their masters. Perhaps it was this difficulty that impelled Rabbi Abulafia to apply the Talmud's distinction between dogs and cats to the realm of religious devotion, rather than mere loyalty to a human owner.

For all his efforts to defend the existence of feline domesticity, Rabbi Henokh Zundel could not refrain from pointing out a decisive difference between the respective forms and degrees of allegiance that are manifested in the two species: When all is said and done, the cat's primary loyalty is to a place rather than to a person. The truth of this assertion can be verified in cases where the master moves to a new dwelling. While a dog will faithfully follow its human to a different place of residence, the cat is just as likely to forsake the master and remain in the old environment to which it has grown accustomed.

Another commentator to the passage, Rabbi Jacob Reischer, took a different approach to describing the supposed spirituality of dogs. In his view, the distinguishing characteristic of dogs is their poverty—I suppose that his personal acquaintance with the species involved junkyard mutts rather than pampered thoroughbreds or lapdogs.

At any rate, Rabbi Reischer explained that there is nothing like poverty for maintaining a community's constant awareness of their dependence on their Creator. This is a sentiment that can be supported from numerous quotations in the Bible and rabbinic works, where affluence is condemned as a factor that impedes piety. He cited an adage from the Talmud to the effect that "poverty is as becoming to Israel as a red strap on the neck of a white horse." Owing to their shared predispositions towards poverty, Jews and dogs have therefore come to share a consciousness of their existential reliance on a higher power.

Page from 18th-century illuminated manuscript of Perek Shirah

It is therefore fitting, says Rabbi Reischer, that the *Perek Shirah*, an ancient work that identifies appropriate songs of praise to be recited by each of nature's creatures, had dogs intoning the words of the Psalm, "Oh come, let us worship and bow down; Let us kneel before the Lord our Maker."

The interpretations that we have been discussing so far offer intriguing readings of the texts, along with some illuminating insights into canine, feline and human characters. Nevertheless, they all suffer from a major shortcoming: they quote the Talmud passage out of context and in an incomplete form.

The full text reads as follows:

> Rabbi Eleazar ben Zadok's disciples asked him: Why does a dog recognize its master while a cat does not recognize its master?
>
> He said to them: Since a person who partakes of something from which a mouse has eaten suffers memory loss—how much more should this apply to one that actually eats the mouse!

Rabbi Eleazar thus focuses not so much on the canine virtues as on the feline diet. Mice were presumed to have poor memories on account of the food that they consumed; and the cats, because of the higher rung they occupy on the food chain, ingest an amnesiac ingredient whenever they gobble up their rodent snacks. This causes them to forget all sorts of things, not just the identities of their masters.

Rabbi Loeb of Prague, the Maharal, was one of the few commentators to cite the Talmud passage in its entirety. However, he too refused to accept it at its face value. The Maharal insisted that the cats' memory problems are not the result of their appetite for mice; for if that were the case, then a cat who has not eaten mice should be immune, which does not seem to be the case.

Rather, the felines' indiscriminate readiness to devour rodents is a symptom of their dismal spiritual state. Mice occupy one of the lowest rungs in the hierarchy of creation, and a being that would eat them has demonstrated thereby the perverse quality of its soul. Rabbi Loeb is careful to stress that what he is talking about has nothing to do with the animals' intelligence, and that he is not accusing cats of stupidity. It is, rather, a matter of their spiritual makeup.

Thus, presumably, while we would be hard put arguing that dogs are smarter than cats, it is somewhat easier to credit them with fine moral qualities like loyalty and courage.

The grave of the Maharal of Prague

Bibliography:

Aptowitzer, Victor. "The Rewarding and Punishing of Animals and Inanimate Objects: On the Aggadic View of the World." *Hebrew Union College Annual* 3 (1926): 117–55.

Isaacs, Ronald H. *Animals in Jewish Thought and Tradition*. Northvale, NJ: Jason Aronson, 2000.

Lawee, Eric. "The Sins of the Fauna in Midrash, Rashi, and Their Medieval Interlocutors." *Jewish Studies Quarterly* 17, no. 1 (2010): 56–98.

Schochet, Elijah Judah. *Animal Life in Jewish Tradition: Attitudes and Relationships*. New York: Ktav, 1984.

Schwartz, Joshua. "Cats in Ancient Jewish Society." *Journal of Jewish Studies* 52, no. 2 (2001): 211–34.

———. "Dogs in Jewish Society in the Second Temple Period and in the Time of the Mishnah and Talmud." *Journal of Jewish Studies* 55, no. 2 (2004): 246–77.

Slifkin, Natan. *Man and Beast: Our Relationships with Animals in Jewish Law and Thought*. Brooklyn: Yashar Books, 2006.

Zellentin, Holger M. *Rabbinic Parodies of Jewish and Christian Literature*. Texte Und Studien Zum Antiken Judentum; Texts and Studies in Ancient Judaism 139. Tübingen: Mohr Siebeck, 2011.

The Messiah Takes Manhattan

A useful rule of thumb in the teaching of Jewish history states that there is generally a correlation between the severity of the troubles besetting the Jews and the intensity of their yearning and expectations for the the coming of messianic redemption. Another rule holds that very few people at any given point in history believed that the world-as-we-know-it would continue for more than fifty years after the current date.

A corollary of all this is that Jews who lived in political and social tranquility were unlikely to be thinking very much about the advent of the redeemer or the restoration of the glory of Israel. This should apply to communities such as that of eighteenth-century America where the small congregations of Jews were being granted true civil rights and enjoying the prosperity that blossomed in the New World.

The fact is that we have relatively sparse information about what American Jews were thinking in those days. They had not reached a state of scholarly erudition that would generate learned tomes by home-grown religious scholars; and the feelings of average Jews in the street were unlikely to get recorded for posterity. In the present instance, however, we do have some fascinating testimony from a prominent American thinker who took a special interest in developments among his Jewish neighbours.

Illustration 1: Ezra Stiles

The witness in question was Ezra Stiles (1727-1795), an illustrious New England educator and theologian who served as President of Yale University and was a founder of Brown University. Like many of his Christian contemporaries, Stiles studied and taught the Hebrew language. He delivered some of his important academic speeches in Hebrew, and may have been responsible for emblazoning the Hebrew words *"Urim v'Thummim"* on Yale's official seal. For more than twenty years he served as a Congregationalist minister in Newport Rhode Island where he maintained close ties with the city's Jewish community. He studied Hebrew Bible and Kabbalah with Rabbi Hayyim Isaac Carregal during the latter's brief sojourn in Newport as an emissary from the holy land, and they afterwards continued to correspond in Hebrew.

Stiles kept a "Literary Diary" which he continued to update with admirable diligence. In the entry for July 26, 1769 he wrote about a friend who "tells me that the Jews in New York expected the Messiah 1768, and are greatly disappointed." It was explained that this messianic expectation had been inspired by a computation of prophetic numbers "by the Rabbins of the present day." This episode seems to be linked to another piece of information that he tossed into the diary: "that two Jews from Constantinople visited New York last year." We might recall that a century earlier, Constantinople had been a main hub of activities for the messianic movement of Shabbetai Zvi.

In his August 10 entry, Stiles recorded a more precise calculation that resulted in the proposal of a somewhat later year for the approaching redemption. A Jewish acquaintance showed him a computation by "one of the present Rabbins of Germany." Like many such calculations, it was based on an enigmatic text from the book of Daniel in which it is stated that the period until the ultimate fulfilment of the great divine wonders will consist of "a time, times, and half a time." According to the unidentified Rabbi, this cryptic expression represents the time that will have elapsed from the destruction of the Second Temple until its restoration and the return of all the tribes of Israel. The unit by which it is measured is a "time"—that is to say, seventy sabbatical cycles adding up to 490 years. Thus, one "time" equals 490 years, "times" is double that or 980 years, while the "half" consists of 245 years, producing a total of 1,715 years. Add that to the date of the Temple's fall (for the calculation to work out, they had to place the event at 68 rather than the accepted historical date 70 C.E.), and that brings us to the year 1783 C.E. The anticipation of the Messiah's advent at that time became a major focus of the religious fervor of Jews in New York.

We may get a tangible picture of how intense this expectation was from another detail in Stiles' diary. He wrote that during thunderstorms the Jews were accustomed keep all their doors and windows open for the coming of the Messiah. This was evident at the time of a violent hail-storm in Newport, during which the Jews "threw open Doors, Windows, and employed themselves in Singing & repeating Prayers, &c., for Meeting Messias."

On the other hand, Stiles told of a conversation he had with a visiting Jew from Poland who, when asked to comment on the German rabbi's messianic computations, simply smiled and said that they await him every day.

The strong impact of this messianic calculation is corroborated by a text written by Rev. Gershom Mendes Seixas, who served at the time as cantor in New York. In addition to a more detailed version of the "time, times and a half" computation, Seixas mentioned two additional calculations. One of them was based on the period of time that the biblical Israelites were steeped in idol-worship, fixed at 245 years. Scripture states that this grave sin is to be punished sevenfold, which produces the same total of 1,715 that served as the foundation for the previous computation. A third calculation mentioned by Ḥazan Seixas divides up the three numbers into distinct historical eras. The "time" of 490 years after the Temple's destruction brings us to 558, marked by the appearance of "the Turkish empire" [that is: the advent of Islam]. Add to that the "times"—980 years—and we are now in 1538 and the Protestant Reformation. The subsequent "half-time" of 245 years should coincide with the Messiah's arrival in 1783, which will bring about redemption for all humanity.

The American Jewish interest in redemption appeared to focus principally on the ingathering of the exiles (an interest that they shared with Christian neighbours). This was a natural sentiment for a community that was largely descended from Spanish and Portuguese exiles who must have felt acutely conscious of their geographic isolation from the centres of mainstream civilization.

Gershom Mendes Seixas (1745–1816)

American Jews were quick to relate to any reports about "exotic" Jewish communities, which they viewed as harbingers of the reunification of the lost tribes of Israel; and they tried to initiate correspondences with coreligionists in far-flung lands like Malabar, India or Kaifeng, China. Their interest in the future ingathering was also sparked by frequent visits from emissaries and fund-raisers from the holy land who were adept at persuading the Jews of the diaspora that they would all shortly be led back to their beloved homeland.

Then as now, anticipating the messiah's arrival was a job that could demand a high price in faith and in soothing the constant disappointments.

But as the old quip has it: the work is steady.

Bibliography:

Baron, Salo Wittmayer. *Palestinian Messengers in America, 1849-79: [a Record of Four Journeys]*. Edited by Jeannette Meisel Baron. America and the Holy Land. New York: Arno Press, 1977.

———. *Steeled by Adversity: Essays and Addresses on American Jewish Life*. Edited by Jeannette Meisel Baron. [1st ed.]. Philadelphia: Jewish Publication Society of America, 1971.

Chiel, Arthur A. "Ezra Stiles and the Jews: A Study in Ambivalence." In *Hebrew and the Bible in America*, edited by Shalom Goldman, 156–167. Hanover, NH: University Press of New England, 1993.

Holmes, Abiel. *The Life of Ezra Stiles*. Boston: Thomas & Andrews, 1798.

Jastrow, Morris. "References to Jews in the Diary of Ezra Stiles." *Publications of the American Jewish Historical Society* 10 (1902): 5–36.

Kohut, George Alexander. *Ezra Stiles and the Jews: Selected Passages from His Literary Diary Concerning Jews and Judaism*. New York: P. Cowen, 1902.

Mahler, Raphael. "American Jewry and the Idea of the Return to Zion in the Period of the American Revolution." *Zion* 15 (1950): 106–143.

Sarna, Jonathan D. "The Mystical World of Colonial American Jew." In *Mediating Modernity: Essays in Honor of Michael A. Meyer.*, edited by Lauren B. Strauss and Michael Brenner, 185–94. Detroit: Wayne State University Press, 2008.

———. "Port Jews in the Atlantic: Further Thoughts." *Jewish History* 20 (2006): 213–19.

Ladies of Letters

I suppose that as long as society requires people to submit letters for various purposes—applications, resumés, recommendations, business correspondence, requests for money or avowals of love—there will exist a market for expert guides to elegant letter-writing; including templates or sample letters. This was especially true in societies where "proper" correspondence was not written in the vernacular language, but in a special literary tongue. For pre-modern Jews this required considerable skill and erudition in Hebrew. This was not limited to mastery of grammar and vocabulary, but in keeping with the accepted conventions, it demanded an erudition that enabled frequent quotes and allusions to passages from the Bible, Talmud and Midrash.

One such collection of writing samples was published in 1533 by Rabbi Samuel Archivolti of Padua (c. 1530–1611) under the title *Ma'ayan Gannim* ["Fountain of Gardens"]. This work was no mere utilitarian assortment of sample correspondence, but included some very specific content. It provided not only the texts of the letters, but also of replies to them. This would seem to imply that both parties to the correspondence were expected to be making use of Rabbi Archivolti's manual; or perhaps, that at least some of the letters in the volume were records of exchanges that had actually taken place. It is also quite possible that the author was merely employing the epistolary format as a fictitious literary device for conveying his personal views.

The fifth and last section of the book was devoted to correspondence between men and women. And one pair of letters there takes the form of a request that was directed by a lady named Dinah to a knowledgeable man, asking him for for advice concerning her pursuit of advanced religious studies. In the flowery Hebrew typical of the era, the lady describes her desire to fulfill this supreme Jewish religious goal, although she is cognizant of the obstacles placed in her way by traditional religious law.

The reply relates seriously to her dilemma. The advisor is impressed with her intellectual qualifications and the purity of her motives; but he cannot ignore the rulings of all those major halakhic authorities who upheld the strict position of Rabbi Eliezer in the Talmud, that "if a man instructs his daughter in Torah, it is as if he were teaching her "*tiflut*"—a Hebrew term that has been given a broad range of translations from "frivolity" to "lewdness." The correspondent is deeply aware of the frustrating contrast between the woman's indisputable worthiness and the talmudic law's abstruseness. In the end, he suggests that the prohibition was directed only at fathers teaching Torah to young girls who would treat the material flippantly, but not to responsible, mature ladies who are capable of coping seriously with the rabbinic curriculum.

Rabbi Archivolti's very specialized manual did not enjoy very wide circulation outside of Italy; and yet after centuries of virtual oblivion, it came to attract a renewed interest in the nineteenth century—this, at least was true for those two letters dealing with women's education.

The best-known instance was in the popular Bible commentary "*Torah Temimah*" by Baruch Epstein of Lithuania. After citing the standard rabbinic rulings that the Torah's instruction to "teach them to your sons" is meant to actively exclude daughters from Torah learning, the Torah Temimah brings Rabbi Archivolti's ingeniously permissive interpretation. Interestingly, he cites it as a "responsum"—a formal legal ruling— without mentioning that it really originated in a letter-writing manual that carried no legal authority, even though it was written by a respected scholar. In fact, Epstein commented that he was really unfamiliar with that rare and obscure book or its author other than to note that

Rabbi Archivolti had been cited as a grammarian in Rabbi Yom-Tov Lipmann Heller's influential commentary to the Mishnah.

All this is quite surprising, to say the least. Rabbi Epstein mentioned the same passage from *Ma'ayan Gannim* in one of the most memorable chapters in his autobiographical memoir, *Mekor Barukh*. The chapter tells of his encounters with his remarkable aunt Rayna Batya Berlin, scion of a distinguished rabbinic dynasty and wife of rabbi Naftali Zvi Yehuda Berlin (known by his acronym the "Netziv") who stood at the helm of the prestigious Volozhin Yeshiva in Lithuania in the nineteenth century.

As a student in his teens, Epstein spent much time in his uncle's home, and his memoir describes Rayna Batya as a well educated lady immersed in tomes of religious scholarship and in general culture (and correspondingly inept in the kitchen). In their frequent conversations on scholarly matters, she took a particular interest in the sources that defined women's roles in rabbinic law and culture, and was very displeased with those roles (which were inferior to those allowed to biblical women). As she stated bitterly, the most ignorant male could bless God for "not making me a woman," to which intelligent, pious woman are obliged to respond "Amen." In their last conversation, his aunt lamented that Jewish women are oppressed and disgraced, but there was no apparent alternative to accepting their regrettable lot in life. (Not unexpectedly, this episode has been heavily bowdlerized in the English version of Rabbi Epstein's memoir issued by an Orthodox publisher, in order to harmonize it with the prevalent atmosphere of fundamentalism.)

Epstein wrote that in one of those conversations, Rayna Batya Berlin cited the letter from Archivolti's *Ma'ayan Gannim* with its suggested solution to the prohibition of women's Torah study; and Epstein relates that he tried to refute her by pointing out that the book was not an actual halakhic work. And yet this, we might recall, was the very same work that he would cite later on in his Torah commentary as a halakhic "responsum," albeit an obscure one with which he was not familiar.

At any rate it is now undeniably clear that neither the Rebitzen Berlin nor Baruch Epstein had access to the original text of Rabbi Archivolti's work; and that Epstein was citing an excerpt that had appeared in the September 25 1895 issue of the Hebrew daily "*Hazefirah*" where the unnamed editor had introduced it as "a letter worthy of publication on account of the position it takes regarding the education of women." This was much later than the alleged conversation with his aunt that Epstein described in his memoir.

Based on this and other evidence, recent scholarship has generally been quite dismissive about the historical veracity of the story, and has concluded that—though the basic description of Mrs. Berlin's personality is probably quite credible—Epstein took extensive literary license in his narrative depiction.

Whatever doubts might arise with respect to the authenticity of Epstein's use of the *Ma'ayan Gannim* letter, it did have the result of introducing an otherwise forgotten source into the contemporary discourse about the schooling of women in Jewish traditionalist circles.

Truly, when we observe the many excellent educational institutions that have been proliferating in recent decades offering intense programs in Torah study for religious women, we are reminded of the visionary words of our sixteenth-century Italian author who wrote: "Those women who are strongly motivated to approach this divine labour as a free and virtuous choice. They will ascend the mountain of the Lord and they will dwell in his holy place, for they are exemplary women. It is therefore fitting that the sages of their generation should praise them, encourage them, inspire them, direct them, strengthen their hands and fortify their arms."

And turning to his correspondent, the aspiring scholar Dinah, he urges (and we are tempted to join in): "Do it and succeed—and you will receive assistance from Heaven!"

Bibliography

Adler, Eliyana R. "Reading Rayna Batya: The Rebellious Rebbetzin as Self-Reflection." *Nashim: A Journal of Jewish Women's Studies & Gender Issues*, no. 16 (2008): 130–52. doi:10.2979/nas.2008.-.16.130.

Assaf, Simcha. *Meḵorot le-Toldhot ha-Ḥinukh be-Yiśra'el*. Edited by Shmuel Glick. Revised and Expanded edition. Vol. 2. 6 vols. New York and Jerusalem: The Jewish Theological Seminary of America, 2001.

Bonfil, Robert. *Jewish Life in Renaissance Italy*. Translated by Anthony Oldcorn. Berkeley: University of California Press, 1994.

Epstein, Baruch. *My Uncle the Netziv*. 1st edition. Brooklyn, NY: Mesorah Publications, 1988.

Fuchs, Ilan. *Jewish Women's Torah Study: Orthodox Religious Education and Modernity*. Routledge Jewish Studies Series. London and New York: Routledge, Taylor & Francis Group, 2014.

———. "Talmud Torah le-Nashim be-'Iṭalia bImei ha-Beinayim U-Vreshit Ha 'Et Ha-Ḥadashah: Sheloshah Diyyunim Hilkhatiyyim." *Massehet* 8 (2009): 29–49. [Hebrew]

Moseley, Marcus. *Being for Myself Alone: Origins of Jewish Autobiography*. Stanford, Calif: Stanford University Press, 2006.

Dan Rabinowitz, "Rayna Batya and Other Learned Women: A Reevaluation of Rabbi Barukh Halevi Epstein's Sources," *Tradition: A Journal of Orthodox Jewish Thought* 35, no. 1 (2001): 55–69.Schwartz, Dror. "R. Samuel Archivolti: His Life, Writings, Responsa and Letters." *Asufot: Annual for Jewish Studies* 7 (1993): 69–156.

Seeman, Don. "The Silence of Rayna Batya: Torah, Suffering, and Rabbi Barukh Epstein's 'Wisdom of Women.'" *The Torah U-Madda Journal* 6 (1995): 91–128.

Shapiro, Marc B. *Changing the Immutable: How Orthodox Judaism Rewrites Its History*. Oxford and Portland, OR: Littman Library of Jewish Civilization, 2015.

———. "Clarifications of Previous Posts." Blog. *The Seforim Blog*, January 16, 2008. http://seforim.blogspot.ca/2008/01/clarifications-of-previous-posts-by.html.

Zinberg, Israel. *Italian Jewry in the Renaissance Era*. Translated by Bernard Martin. A History of Jewish Literature. Cincinnati and New York: Hebrew Union College Press and KTAV, 1988.

Rabbis, Rationalists...and a Remedy that Roars

Last year I experienced the excruciating agony of a kidney stone. Fortunately, I was in Jerusalem at the time and had access to capable Israeli medical professionals (as well as generous Canadian medical insurance), and by the time the first round of painkillers wore off, the stone was gone.

If the stone had stricken me in thirteenth-century Europe, I might have sought a different form of treatment: namely, the application of a "lion medallion," This procedure took the form of a specially prepared metal disk (crafted during a particular phase of the moon) engraved with the zodiac sign of Leo the lion. This medallion was strapped over the offending kidney in order to relieve the pain. The device was supposed to help by beaming down therapeutic forces from the stars.

This procedure was widely recommended by physicians in the Languedoc region of what is now southern France. There were many distinguished Jewish rationalists and scientists in that age who believed in the efficacy of "astral magic"—the theory that the celestial bodies radiate energies whose effects can be calculated mathematically and astronomically. Advocates of the theory included respected scholars of the stature of Abraham Ibn Ezra. On the other hand, Moses Maimonides had famously discredited the pseudoscience, branding all astrology as intrinsically idolatrous--and the Languedocian Jews were stalwart in their adulation of Maimonides.

Nonetheless, the Provençal physician Isaac de Lattes was accustomed to preparing these medallions at the requests of his patients, though he personally was not a believer in astrology. Dr. de Lattes regretted employing this questionable treatment and he feared that it might be forbidden on religious grounds—even if somehow it were medically beneficial. He therefore addressed an inquiry to Rabbi Solomon ben Adret of Barcelona—the Rashba— perhaps the most respected halakhic authority of that generation, and the Rashba ruled that the treatment was permissible.

This arcane question concerning the medical use of the Leo medallions would soon became a contentious issue in a major ideological dispute between the rabbis of Languedoc and Catalonia over the spiritual directions of their Jewish communities.

The controversy erupted when preachers in Montpellier, a community that was deeply devoted to Maimonides' rationalist vision of Judaism, began to base their sermons on allegorical interpretations of the Bible that might be construed as denying the literal truth of scripture. Though no one was questioning the importance of philosophical and scientific study in the quest for theological truth, some of the community's leaders were worried that rationalist ideas would be misunderstood by younger folk who did not yet have adequate background in the traditional Jewish religious curriculum. Therefore, conservative elements sought to issue a communal ordinance forbidding the preaching of allegorical sermons to the general public, and limiting the study of metaphysics to those above the age of thirty.

With those objectives in mind, Rabbi Abba Mari ben Joseph Yarḥi turned to Rabbi Ibn Adret asking him to throw his considerable prestige behind such an ordinance. Rashba was known to be rather unsympathetic to Maimonides' Aristotelian rationalism—he was in fact an exponent of the emerging mystical doctrine of Kabbalah.

In his initial letter of invitation to the Barcelonan sage, Abba Mari inserted what appears to be a completely irrelevant reference to the Leo medallions. Although the letter's overriding tone was one of obsequious humility in which the writer was begging for a favour from his intellectual and spiritual superior, Abba Mari included a provocative question about how Rashba could ever have permitted the use of astrological medallions.

The Provençal rabbi subsequently tried to explain that the two issues were indeed unrelated, but they happened to come to his attention around the same time. Historians, however, have generally preferred to see it as part of a deliberate strategy. Knowing that many loyal Languedocian Jews resented his turning to an outside authority to challenge the proud local culture, Abba Mari took advantage of this opportunity to demonstrate that he was not submitting meekly to the Rashba's authority; where warranted, he was prepared to voice his opposition on an issue that was dear to the hearts of his community.

Abba Mari boldly took Rashba to task for his permissive ruling on the medical medallions. He argued that this was an unmistakable transgression of a severe prohibition in the Torah: "Do not practice divination or seek omens," which the Talmud interpreted as forbidding astrological computations.

Leo Sigil in 1763 letter (Copyright © The Royal Society)

Rashba was able to hold his own in the debate, in both his rabbinic erudition and his competence in scientific theory. He cited a passage from the Talmud that allowed the placing of engraved coins on foot calluses on the Sabbath, indicating that our sages did not object to the medical use of such engraved images. He also argued that there is nothing theologically unacceptable about the premise that the Almighty might have structured the cosmos in such a way that certain material objects possess healing properties (even though science cannot necessarily explain them). As long as one's intentions when using the medallion are directed to its medical efficacy and not to any superstitious or idolatrous powers that are mistakenly ascribed to it, then there should be nothing objectionable in resorting to such treatment. As it happens, similar debates were going on at the same time among their Christian neighbours. For example, Paris's Bishop William of Auvergne was careful to differentiate between cures that were founded on superstitious or demonic beliefs in the images, as distinct from therapies that had a real "scientific" basis.

In discussing the sources for the Leo medallions, Rabbi Abba Mari mentioned the existence of a "Book of Forms" in Hebrew that contained diagrams and instructions for fashioning medallions of the zodiac signs. Scholars have expended considerable efforts in tracking down this volume.

In those days Montpellier was the focus of intense interreligious cooperation and collaboration in medical science, and prominent Christian scholars were translating treatises from the Hebrew (many of which had in turn been translated by Jewish doctors from Arabic originals). Prominent in these circles was the prolific physician, translator and religious reformer Arnald of Villanova. Arnald was the probable author of a work known as "De Sigillis," a detailed guide to the fashioning of medical medallions based on the twelve signs of the zodiac. The treatise specified the appropriate timing, materials, inscriptions and accompanying blessings; as well as which physical ailments could be treated by each sign. In July 1301 Arnald used a lion medallion to alleviate the pain of a kidney stone for no less a celebrity than Pope Boniface VIII, an episode that raised some eyebrows among the cardinals. Another Latin treatise about the medical uses of zodiac medallions was authored by the Montpellier physician Bernard de Gordon.

Arnald of Villanova

Both those texts stipulated that the medallion—preferably one fashioned out of gold on a sunny day and fumigated with mastic—should be applied to the left kidney, that the lion should have no tongue and that a veiled lady wielding a rod or bridle should be riding on it.

These manuals were likely derived in turn from an Arabic original, the influential eleventh century compendium of magic and astrology "*Ghayat al-Ḥakim*" known in its European translations as "the Picatrix."

I assume that most of us would not give much credence to any snake-oil peddler who tried to prescribe zodiac medallions as the remedy for what ails us.

But if the pain becomes unbearably acute, even some of us skeptics might become more receptive to such unconventional treatments.

After all—like a dose of good chicken soup—it can't hurt...

Bibliography:

Baer, Yitzhak. *A History of the Jews in Christian Spain*. Philadelphia: Jewish Publication Society, 1992.

Caballero-Navas, Carmen. "Medicine among Medieval Jews: The Science, the Art, and the Practice." In *Science in Medieval Jewish Cultures*, edited by Gad Freudenthal, 320–42. New York: Cambridge University Press, 2011.

Delmas, Bruno. "Médailles astrologiques et talismaniques dans le Midi de la France (XIIIe-XIVe siècle)." In *Archéologie Occitaine*, 237–54. Paris: Bibliothèque nationale, 1976. [French]

Halbertal, Moshe. *Between Torah and Wisdom: Rabbi Menachem Ha-Meiri and the Maimonidean Halakhists in Provence*. Jerusalem: Magnes Press, 2000. [Hebrew]

Klein-Braslavy, Sara. "The Concept of Magic in R. Solomon Ben Abraham Adret (Rashba) and R. Nissim Gerondi (Ran)." In *"Encuentros" and "Desencuentros"; Spanish Jewish Cultural Interaction throughout History: The Howard Gilman International Symposia, Harvard, Salamanca, Tel-Aviv*, edited by Carlos Carrete Parrondo, 105–29. Tel-Aviv: University Publishing Projects, 2000.

Kottek, Samuel. "Le Symbole du Lion dans la Médicine de l'Antiquité et du Moyen Age." *Revue d'histoire de la médecine hébraïque*. 20 (1967): 161–68. [French]

Lang, Benedek. "Characters and Magic Signs in the Picatrix and Other Medieval Magic Texts." *Acta Classica Universitatis Scientiarum Debreceniensis* 47 (2011): 69–77.

Renan, Ernest. *Les Rabbins Français Du Commencement Du Quatorzième Siècle*. Paris: Imprimerie Nationale, 1877. [French]

Pingree, David Edwin, ed. *Picatrix: The Latin Version of the "Ghāyat Al-Hakīm."* Studies of the Warburg Institute. London: Warburg Inst, 1986.

Roos, Anna Marie. "'Magic Coins' and 'Magic Squares': The Discovery of Astrological Sigils in the Oldenburg Letters." *Notes & Records of the Royal Society* 62, no. 3 (September 20, 2008): 271–88.

Schwartz, Dov. *Studies on Astral Magic in Medieval Jewish Thought*. Translated by David Louvish and Batya Stein. The Brill Reference Library of Judaism, v. 20. Leiden: Brill-Styx, 2004.

Shatzmiller, Joseph. "In Search of the 'Book of Figures': Medicine and Astrology in Montpellier at the Turn of the Fourteenth Century." *AJS Review* 7–8 (1982): 383–407.

———. "The Forms of the Twelve Constellations: A 14th Century Controversy." *Jerusalem Studies in Jewish Thought* 9 (1990): 397–408.

Stern, Gregg. *Philosophy and Rabbinic Culture: Jewish Interpretation and Controversy in Medieval Languedoc*. Routledge, 2013.

By the Time We Get to Phoenix

Among the multitudes of my devoted readers I suppose there are probably a few bird-watchers. And I would also hazard a guess that, however many species of winged creatures they might have seen—not one of them has ever sighted a phoenix.

Nevertheless, stories about this extraordinary bird can be traced back to the most ancient records of human culture.

Hesiod in a detail from a mosaic by Monnus

Roman copy (2nd century C.E.) of a Greek bust of Herodotus

A fragment attributed to the Greek writer Hesiod who lived around 700 B.C.E. spoke of the phoenix's impressive life-span—nine times that of the long-lived raven. Several centuries later, the historian Herodotus provided considerably more detail about the phoenix—though to be sure, he did not claim to have seen one (other than in a painting), nor did he guarantee the veracity of the tales he was repeating. Herodotus' description contains most of the elements that subsequently became standard features of the "phoenix legend." For example, the birds are dazzlingly coloured, with plumage of red and gold; and they are as large as eagles.

Herodotus' phoenix makes only the very rarest of appearances to the inhabited world, at intervals of no less than five hundred years. Their arrivals coincide with the deaths of their parents. The young phoenix takes care of the funeral rites for its deceased parent, conveying the corpse from Arabia to the Egyptian temple of the sun at Heliopolis where it covers the deceased body in fragrant myrrh and performs a complex rite with an egg-shaped lump of myrrh. This later came to be perceived as a single process of resurrection in which the selfsame bird was restored to life in a newly regenerated body.

This quintessentially pagan legend, which probably arose out of the rich mythological traditions of Egypt, was well known to Jewish writers in the ancient world. Some Jewish Apocalyptic visions contain fantastic descriptions of phoenixes that were observed by their mystic heroes as they ascended toward the sublime throne of the Almighty.

A Jewish playwright known as Ezekiel the Tragedian (second century B.C.E.) composed a Greek play about the Exodus (known as the "Exagogé"), portions of which have survived in quotations by later authors. One of those fragments relates to an obscure episode in the Torah, shortly after the parting of the Red Sea and the miraculous sweetening of the bitter waters at Marah, when the Israelites encamped at an oasis named Elim which provided them with twelve wells of water and seventy date palms. Ezekiel's script contains a speech by the scout who reported to Moses on discovering this idyllic spot, and his description includes a sighting of a huge multi-coloured bird (the word "phoenix" does not actually appear in the text) twice the size of an eagle, with an exceptional voice, who comported himself like the king of the birds and was treated as such by the other birds.

The Phoenix being reborn, from a medieval Latin manuscript in the British Library

Not enough of the text remains to let us figure out why the play's author was impelled to insert this detail, one that does not seem to be suggested by the wording of biblical narrative. There are indications that a tradition existed about an appearance of the phoenix during the reign of the Pharaoh Amasis who was believed to have lived at the time of the Exodus. This would be consistent with the view that was widely held among the ancients, that great epochs and historical turning-points (and from the Jewish perspective, the Israelite liberation from slavery and the revelation at Mount Sinai would surely qualify as such) were marked by sightings of the phoenix. Indeed, a large portion of the literature about the phoenix was devoted to measuring its life-span and calculating the dates of its past and future rebirths.

Ezekiel's insertion of the phoenix episode into the biblical story might also have something to do with the date-palms that flourished in Elim. The Greek word for date-palm is also "phoenix," and this has given rise to several scholarly disagreements about the meanings of various texts in which the word appears.

This confusion extended to passages in the Bible. The familiar verse in Psalms that "the righteous shall flourish like the palm tree" was translated by some Christian exegetes (including the Latin Vulgate version) as "like the *phoenix*." Indeed, in Christian art and homiletics, the phoenix became a favourite symbol and precedent for the doctrine of the resurrection of the dead.

Rabbinic tradition also discerned several references to phoenixes in the Bible. One of these texts was a verse in the book of Job in which the hero recalls his happier and more hope-filled days: "Then I said, I shall die in my nest, and I shall multiply my days as the sand." The Hebrew word (*ḥol*) that is translated here according to its normal sense of "sand" was understood by some rabbis as the name of a bird; and in fact, an alternative Masoretic tradition read it with a different vowel, as "*ḥul*"; this interpretation is preferred by several modern scholars. The Alexandrian Greek translation translated the text as "the trunk of a palm tree," using that ambiguous word "phoenix."

A tradition in the midrash teaches that when Eve ate the forbidden fruit, she also offered to share it with all her fellow-creatures in the garden of Eden, and the only one to decline the offer was the virtuous *ḥol* bird—for which it was rewarded with a blessing of longevity or immortality. In this respect it differed from the other, less disciplined creatures who were, like the humans, deprived of their primordial immortality.

Rabbis from the early third century explained the phoenix's immortality in terms that dovetailed with Greek traditions about its lifespan. They said that it lives for a thousand years, at the conclusion of which, according to one view, a flame emerges from its nest and burns it up completely, leaving an egg from which it regenerates limbs and springs back to life; and according to a second theory, the aged bird's body simply decays without the sudden fiery conflagration, and is then recreated.

These two theories about the regeneration of the *ḥol* bird correspond precisely with the two dominant Greek traditions about the process of the phoenix's rebirth. The egg motif had become a standard element of the myth since Herodotus. The image of the new phoenix arising from the flames of the old has of course become the most popular version and is frequently invoked as a metaphor.

Some commentators also claimed that there was a phoenix on the passenger list of Noah's ark. The Talmud quotes a conversation in which Noah's son Shem chatted with Abraham's servant Eliezer about the grueling workload faced by his father when catering to the individual needs of all the diverse denizens of that floating zoo. One of those creatures, designated by the (otherwise unknown) name "avarshana" or "urshana," lay uncomplainingly in a corner of the vessel. When Noah tried to offer him food, the humble avarshana replied that he hadn't wanted to trouble his host who seemed so busy with his other onerous chores. Noah was so impressed with its considerateness that he blessed the creature with eternal life. In this connection, the Talmud cited the verse from Job.

Rashi inferred that the avarshana was none other than the phoenix—a thesis that achieved much popularity among subsequent commentators—even though the Babylonian Ge'onim, like most modern lexicographers, preferred to translate it as a more conventional type of bird, likely a dove or pigeon (albeit one capable of carrying on conversations with humans). Interestingly, some ancient Greek writers mentioned that no-one ever observed a phoenix eating.

In the Jewish work known as "the Apocalypse of Baruch," we should note, the phoenix is said to be responsible for using its wings to screen humanity from the deadly rays of direct sunlight—a motif that would also resurface in rabbinic midrashic traditions.

Perhaps its next appearance will bring a solution to global warming and the hole in the ozone layer.

Hopefully we won't have to wait a thousand years—or even five hundred—for that to happen.

Bibliography:

Aptowitzer, Victor. "The Rewarding and Punishing of Animals and Inanimate Objects: On the Aggadic View of the World." *Hebrew Union College Annual* 3 (1926): 117–55.

Broek, Roelof van den. *The Myth of the Phoenix: According to Classical and Early Christian Traditions*. Études Préliminaires Aux Religions Orientales Dans l'Empire Romain 24. Leiden: E. J. Brill, 1971.

Dahood, Mitchell Joseph. "Hol 'Phoenix' in Job 29:18 and in Ugaritic." *The Catholic Biblical Quarterly* 36, no. 1 (1974): 85–88.

———. "Nest and Phoenix in Job 29:18." *Biblica* 48, no. 4 (1967): 542–44.

Ginzberg, Louis. *The Legends of the Jews*. Translated by Henrietta Szold. Philadelphia, PA: The Jewish Publication Society of America, 1909.

Gutman, Yehoshua. *Beginnings of Jewish-Hellenistic Literature*. 2 vols. Jerusalem: Mosad Bialik, 1958. [Hebrew]

Heath, Jane. "Ezekiel Tragicus and Hellenistic Visuality: The Phoenix at Elim." *The Journal of Theological Studies* 57, no. 1 (2006): 23–41.

Hill, John Spencer. "The Phoenix." *Religion & Literature* 16, no. 2 (1984): 61–66.

Hubaux, Jean, and Maxime Leroy. *Le Mythe du Phénix dans les Littératures Grecque et Latine*. Bibliothèque de la Faculté de philosophie et lettres de l'Université de Liège. Fasc. LXXXII. Liège, Paris: Faculté de philosophie et lettres et E. Droz, 1939.

Jacobson, Howard. *The Exagoge of Ezekiel*. Cambridge, [Cambridgeshire]; New York: Cambridge University Press, 1983.

———. "Phoenix Resurrected." *Harvard Theological Review* 80, no. 2 (1987): 229–33.

Kohn, Thomas D. "The Tragedies of Ezekiel." *Greek, Roman, and Byzantine Studies* 43, no. 1 (2011): 5–12.

McDonald, Mary Francis. "Phoenix Redivivus." *Phoenix* 14, no. 4 (1960): 187–206.

Niehoff, Maren R. "The Phoenix in Rabbinic Literature." *Harvard Theological Review* 89, no. 3 (1996): 245–65.

Nigg, Joseph. *The Phoenix: An Unnatural Biography of a Mythical Beast*. University of Chicago Press, 2016.

Petersen, Anders Klostergaard. "Between Old and New: The Problem of Acculturation Illustrated by the Early Christian Use of the Phoenix Motif." In *Jerusalem, Alexandria, Rome: Studies in Ancient Cultural Interaction in Honour of A. Hilhorst*, edited by Florentino García Martinez and Gerald P. Luttikhuizen, 148–64. Leiden and Boston: Brill, 2003.

Slifkin, Nosson. "Sacred Monsters: Mysterious and Mythical Creatures of Scripture, Talmud and Midrash." Brooklyn, N.Y: Zoo Torah, 2007.

Moo-sical Mystics

As the story is told in the Bible, the Philistines in the days of the Prophet Samuel thought they were neutralizing Israel's most effective secret weapon when they captured the ark of the covenant that housed the original tablets of the ten commandments. However, when (not heeding the lessons of Indiana Jones) they found themselves cursed with a plague of tumours, rats, and maybe hemorrhoids, they decided to send the ark back to the Israelites. They placed it on a cart pulled by two milk-cows; and in order to test whether the process was truly being guided by the Hebrew God, they stood watch to observe whether the cows would steer a direct homeward course—and this was indeed what occurred.

According to traditions preserved in the works of Josephus Flavius and the pseudepigraphic "Biblical Antiquities" ascribed to Philo of Alexandria, the cows were placed at the intersection of three roads so that the Philistines could observe whether the heavenly GPS network would direct them to the correct path toward Judea,

Not content with the impressive miracle that was described explicitly in the biblical tale, several rabbis of the Talmud and

The cows pulling the Ark of the Covenant; from the fresco of the ancient Dura Europos synagogue

Midrash looked for allusions to additional layers of supernatural involvement. They read the Hebrew verb "*vayyisharnah*" [= they went straight] as if it were from a similar root meaning "they sang," and this conjured up for them an image of cows singing the praises of the Lord as they pulled the holiest of objects on its way to its real home in the sanctuary of the Lord.

But what does a cow sing while hauling a sacred ark? A diverse roster of sages spanning several generations of the talmudic era, in both the land of Israel and Babylonia, identified appropriate passages from Psalms and other scriptural texts as the bovine librettos. The suggestions included the song that Moses and the Israelites intoned after the splitting of the Red Sea, as well as uplifting thanksgiving hymns like "Sing to the Lord a new song," "The Lord reigns, let the earth be glad," "Sing to the Lord, all the earth, "The Lord reigns, let the nations tremble," or "Give thanks unto the Lord, call upon his name."

The Talmud's playlist also included one selection of lyrics that were not quoted from a biblical source. It was ascribed to the Galilean sage Rabbi Isaac Nappaḥa; and a virtually identical tradition appears in the MIdrash *Genesis Rabbah* in the name of Elijah—presumably, the famous prophet himself. Elijah makes occasional appearances in rabbinic literature in his role as a figure who divided his time between the "heavenly academy" and periodic visits with worthy rabbis on earth. The current passage evidently belongs to a body of traditions known as "*Tanna de-Bei Eliyahu*," some of which are cited in midrashic and talmudic literature, and which formed the basis for a remarkable and enigmatic homiletic compendium that was probably compiled around the tenth century.

The song of the cows, as reported by Rabbi Isaac Nappaḥa or Elijah, went as follows:

> Exalt, exalt, acacia!
>
> Stretch forth in the fulness of thy majesty,

> girdled in golden embroidery,
>
> praised in the recesses of the palace,
>
> resplendent in the finest of ornaments.

And if that sounds to you like an obscure mishmash of cryptic verbiage, then we must bear in mind that this song followed the conventions of classical Hebrew liturgical poetry (*piyyut*). A standard feature of that genre was that fundamental concepts and persons are never named directly, but only hinted at through the use of indirect expressions taken from biblical usage. Thus, in the current example, the mentions of acacia and gold serve as poetic code-words that are supposed to evoke the instructions in the book of Exodus: "they shall make an ark of acacia wood... and thou shalt overlay it with pure gold, within and without shalt thou overlay it, and shalt make upon it a crown of gold round about."

The passage about the singing cows played a significant part in tracing the historical development of Jewish mystical schools. One of those schools, known as "*Heikhalot*," is known from texts that describe mystical ascents through a hierarchy of "palaces" and culminate in a sublime vision of the throne of God as it is borne on an chariot made up of angels. The authors and students of the Heikhalot texts claimed that the mystical disciplines described in them were the same ones that were practiced by the rabbis of the talmudic era. However, because the ancient sages maintained a high degree of reticence regarding this esoteric lore, we possess little explicit testimony about the matter.

Our knowledge of the Heikhalot school and its teachings derives only from documents that stem from the medieval era (though the texts are fictitiously ascribed to ancient rabbis). The normal scholarly policy for determining the dates for such traditions is to exercise maximal skepticism, which would lead, in this case, to the assumption that, until proven otherwise, the phenomenon of Heikhalot mysticism did not exist prior to the medieval documents in which it was recorded.

It turns out, however, that the "acacia" song ascribed to the bovine choir in the Talmud and Midrash bears an extraordinary resemblance to the hymns sung by angelic beings in the Hekhalot literature. The similarity extends to numerous literary qualities of the respective creations, including their vocabulary, their exalted style, and their poetic rhythm.

In light of this extraordinary resemblance, it has been argued that Rabbi Isaac Nappaḥa or Elijah expected their audience to make the thematic association with the mystical Hekhalot hymns. If that is indeed true, then the mystical traditions of the Heikhalot must have been in existence centuries earlier than previously thought—at least as early as the late third century, during the generation of Rabbi Isaac Nappaḥa.

In fact, the placing of a mystical hymn in the mouths of cattle would fit nicely with the central imagery of rabbinic mysticism, which is based largely on Ezekiel's portrayal of the divine Chariot, drawn by inscrutable "holy living creatures." Understood from this perspective, the cows who pulled the ark of the covenant—even though they had ostensibly been provided by the heathen Philistines—were mirroring the celestial creatures of the heavenly entourage.

And yet not all the rabbis were comfortable with the notion of singing cows. The great Babylonian sage Rav Ashi insisted that Rabbi Isaac's hymn had nothing to do with the return of the ark from the Philistines; rather it had been chanted by the (humans) Israelites in connection with a different biblical passage about the ark of the covenant, as described in the book of Numbers: "And it came to pass, when the ark set forward, that Moses said, Rise up, Lord, and let thine enemies be scattered"—the verse that we still sing when removing the Torah scrolls from the synagogue ark.

We may speculate that Rav Ashi was uneasy with an approach that credulously accepted the existence of singing animals, and that it was for this reason that he chose instead to attach the whole discussion to a different (but comparable) context, the travels of the ark through the wilderness during the time of Moses.

Although the wondrous vision of musical cattle seems to have been accepted almost routinely by most of the rabbis who contributed to the discussions, we do find one expression of sheer amazement at the idea—perhaps uttered from the perspective of someone who was personally conversant with the pitfalls of teaching choirs to sing harmoniously.

Thus, Rabbi Samuel bar Nahman addressed the talented cows in wide-eyed admiration and compared them favourably to the Levites who sang in the Temple choirs: "How much toil did the son of Amram [i.e., Moses] need to expend before he could teach the Levites how to sing—and yet you are able to intone the song all by yourselves! Bravo!"

Bibliography:

Aptowitzer, Victor. "The Rewarding and Punishing of Animals and Inanimate Objects: On the Aggadic View of the World." *Hebrew Union College Annual* 3 (1926): 117–55.

Bacher, Wilhelm. *Die Agada der babylonischen Amoräer: Ein Beitrag zur Geschichte der Agada und zur Einleitung in den babylonischen Talmud.* Frankfurt a. M., 1913.

Davila, James. *Descenders to the Chariot: The People Behind the Hekhalot Literature.* Leiden and Boston: Brill, 2001.

Elbaum, Jacob. "The Midrash Tana Devei Eliyahu and Ancient Esoteric Literature." *Jerusalem Studies in Jewish Thought* 6, no. 1–2 (1987): 139–50. [Hebrew]

Fleischer, E. *Hebrew Liturgical Poetry in the Middle Ages.* 2nd expanded edition. Jerusalem: Magnes Press, 2007. [Hebrew]

Friedmann, Meïr, ed. *Seder Eliyahu Rabah.* Jerusalem: Wahrman, 1969. [Hebrew]

Ginzberg, Louis. *Legends of the Jews.* Translated by Henrietta Szold. 2nd ed. Philadelphia: Jewish Publication Society of America, 2003.

Halperin, David J. *The Faces of the Chariot: Early Jewish Responses to Ezekiel's Vision.* Texte Und Studien Zum Antiken Judentum 16. Tübingen: J.C.B. Mohr, 1988.

Lindbeck, Kristen H. *Elijah and the Rabbis: Story and Theology.* New York: Columbia University Press, 2010.

Mann, Jacob. "Date and Place of Redaction of Seder Eliyahu Rabba and Zuṭṭa." *Hebrew Union College Annual* 4 (1927): 302–10.

Scholem, Gershom G. *Jewish Gnosticism, Merkabah Mysticism, and Talmudic Tradition*. New York: Jewish Theological Seminary of America, 1960.

———. *Major Trends in Jewish Mysticism*. New York: Schocken, 1961.

Seidenberg, David Mevorach. *Kabbalah and Ecology: God's Image in the More-Than-Human World*. New York: Cambridge University Press, 2015.

Urbach, Efraim Elimelech. "The Traditions Concerning Mystical Doctrine in the Period of the Tannaim." In *Studies in Mysticism and Religion, Presented to Gershom G. Scholem on his Seventieth Birthday by Pupils, Colleagues and Friends*, edited by Efraim Elimelech Urbach, R. J. Zwi Werblowsky, and Chaim Wirszubski, 1–29. Jerusalem: Magnes Press, 1967. [Hebrew]

Illustration of the Red Heifer from a manuscript of liturgical poetry, probably from Germany, in the British Library

Yellow is the New Red

The longest of the Qur'an's 114 chapters is known as "Surat al-Baḳarah," the Chapter of the Cow. Much of this section consists of re-tellings of episodes from the Torah. The brief passage that gives the chapter its name is not found at the beginning, but well into the chapter, commencing at verse 67. It is quite a memorable passage, and it might sound familiar to people who are conversant with the Bible and with Jewish tradition. And yet, for all its resemblance to the Torah account, it differs from it in important respects.

The passage begins with Moses conveying to the people a divine command to sacrifice a cow. As the Israelites pressed their leader for more clarification, Moses kept piling on additional conditions that were necessary for the cow to qualify for the purpose, overwhelming them with minute specifications that were far more burdensome than anything they had initially imagined. In the end, the prophet informed them that the Almighty will not accept just any cow, but it must be "neither old, nor virgin, midway between the two ages." Its colour should be a bright, pleasant-looking yellow. It must not have been raised either to plow the earth or to irrigate a field, and it was to be free from any blemishes or spots.

Finding such a cow was indeed a more formidable task than they had anticipated, but nevertheless, with considerable reluctance they located an acceptable animal and sacrificed it as instructed.

Several of the expressions that appear in the description of the Qur'an's cow are reminiscent of the passage in the book of Numbers in which God commanded the Israelites to bring "a red heifer without spot, wherein is no blemish, and upon which never came a yoke." In the Torah, this unusual cow—red rather than yellow in hue (though there is some disagreement about how exactly to translate the Arabic word)—is to be slaughtered and burned in its entirety under strictly defined conditions; then its ashes are mixed in living waters along with other ingredients, to be sprinkled as part of the purification ritual for persons who have been rendered impure through contact with a corpse.

In rabbinic discourse, the red heifer became the paradigm for a divine commandment that transcends human comprehension. In the Muslim scripture, however, the purpose of the sacrifice seems more practical. It is linked to the passage immediately following, in which God says to recall "when you slew a man and disputed over it, but God was to bring out that which you were concealing. So, we said: Strike the slain man with part of it."

Unlike the Hebrew text, the Qur'an connects the slaughtering of the cow to a specific incident: an unsolved murder for which the community was held culpable (the Arabic uses the plural form of "you slew"). This suggests that it was equating the law of the red heifer with a different biblical precept, the law of the "broken-necked heifer."

Decoration from the Banberg Maḥzor (Germany, 13th century) in the Jewish Theological Seminary of America

This second precept, found in the book of Deuteronomy, sets out the procedure to be followed when a corpse is discovered outside a town "in the land the Lord your God is giving you to possess" (as distinct from the wilderness where the people were encamped in Moses's time) and the assailant is unknown. The procedure also includes the killing of a "heifer that has never been put to work or worn a yoke." The elders are instructed to break the heifer's neck in a rough valley.

It is common to write off the Qur'an's version as an instance of the ignorant Muhammad confusing two unrelated laws that are dealing with very different situations—one prescribing a ritual for ritual purification after contact with a corpse (one that, in most cases, would have died of natural causes); whereas the other is intended to effect atonement for a serious crime. (Perhaps he was also adding the notorious "golden calf" into his polychromatic palette.) This would be consistent with the historical picture promoted by Islamic tradition, that Muhammad was an illiterate who lived in a remote and religiously isolated society in which barbaric ignorance prevailed—what the Arabs call the "Jahiliyya"—and picked up fragments of religious lore from conversations with diverse informants. Historians now assess the situation rather differently. Arabia in the sixth century was in communication with the foremost civilizations of the time, and Judaism and Christianity were well established there, especially in the town of Yathrib (which would become the Islamic "al-Madinah") where the "Baḳarah" chapter was most likely revealed.

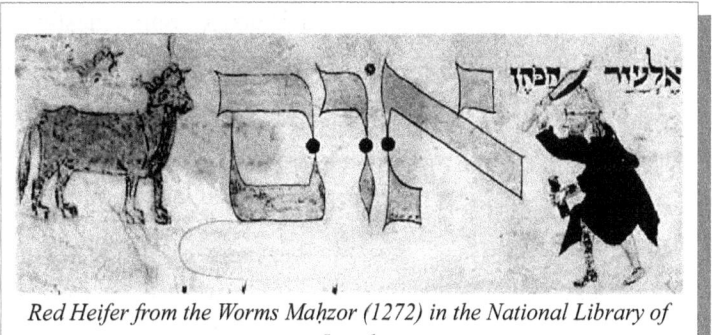

Red Heifer from the Worms Maḥzor (1272) in the National Library of Israel

ooked at more sympathetically, the Qur'an's blending of the diverse texts is reminiscent of rabbinic midrash with its readiness to elicit new meaning from comparisons of similar expressions in otherwise unrelated passages of scripture—by employing the hermeneutical trope known in Hebrew as *gezerah shavah*. Not only are there strong similarities in the attributes of the respective cows used for the Torah's corpse-related laws (in ways that set them apart from any other sacrificial animals), but scripture refers to the red heifer as a "*ḥaṭṭat*"—a sin offering.

Like the rabbinic tradition, the Qur'an was puzzled by the bizarre number of arbitrary-sounding conditions that were attached to the ritual, and it provided a satisfying answer: they were added as a punitive response for the people's raising superfluous questions about what had originally been a straightforward command! I can easily imagine Muhammad being irritated by members of his own nascent community who were wasting his time with such unnecessary questions; or by Jews whom he failed to convert to his faith because the laws of his new religion were not quite detailed or stringent enough for their taste.

Commentators to the Qur'an were pleased to fill in the details of the murder case that prompted the sacrifice of the cow. Most of the scenarios involved greedy heirs killing wealthy relatives and depositing the corpse near somebody else's domain. The commentary ascribed to 'Abd Allah Ibn 'Abbas explained that in such cases, the distance between the dead man and the two towns would be carefully measured—a detail that was undoubtedly derived from Deuteronomy and its Jewish interpreters.

In the Qur'an God commands cryptically to strike the deceased with a part of the cow, presenting this as an example of the resurrection of the dead. The commentaries explained that the victim actually stood up at that point and identified his murderer. At any rate, it is characteristic of the Qur'an to introduce allusions to resurrection at every opportunity, a belief that Islam inherited from Judaism though it has very little explicit basis in the Hebrew scriptures.

Muslim exegetes liked to inflate the exorbitant price that was ultimately paid to acquire the rare "golden heifer"—including the view that they had to fill its hide with gold—whereby its purchase served as a fitting punishment for the disobedient Israelites or for the murderers.

A popular variation on this theme was brought by the exegete Ismail al-Suddi. He recounted a tale about a man who came to a house to sell a pearl; however, the master of the house was napping, so his son conducted the negotiations, arriving at an advantageous price for the jewel. The dutiful son refused to conclude the deal because he did not wish to disturb his father slumber to take

A Red Heifer in an illuminated Bible from Spain in the Bblioteca Nacional, Lisbon

the money. Eventually, God compensated him for his virtuous behaviour by arranging for the precious yellow cow to be born in his herd. When the community tried to purchase the animal from him, they could not come to agreement on the price, and eventually Moses had to intercede and order him to sell it to them for ten times its weight in gold.

Students of rabbinic literature will readily recognize this narrative as a slightly altered version of the Talmud's tale about Dama ben Natina, a pagan in Ashkelon whose devotion to his father's comfort was cited as a model lesson of how to honour one's parents

There is, as we have seen, much to be derived from Moses's mysterious heifer—and the interpreters of the respective scriptures have illuminated those lessons through a prism of vivid colours.

Bibliography:

Friedman, Shamma. "Dama bar Netinah: Li-Dmuto Ha-Historit. Pereq Be-Ḥeqer Ha-Aggadah Ha-Talmudit." In *Higayon L'Yona: New Aspects in the Study of Midrash, Aggadah and Piyut in Honor of Professor Yona Fraenkel*, 83–130. Jerusalem: Magnes Press, 2006. [Hebrew]

Geiger, Abraham. *Judaism and Islam*. The Library of Jewish Classics. New York: Ktav, 1970.

Goldziher, Igńac. *Muslim Studies*. Edited by S. M. Stern. New Brunswick, NJ: Aldine Transaction, 2006.

Katsh, Abraham Isaac. *Judaism in Islām: Biblical and Talmudic Backgrounds of the Koran and Its Commentaries*. 3d ed. The

Judaic Studies Library, no. SHP 5. New York: Sepher-Hermon Press, 1980.

Madelung, Wilferd, and Alan Jones, eds. *The Commentary on the Qur'ān by Abū Ja'far Muḥammad B. Jarīr Al-Ṭabarī.* Translated by John Cooper. Oxford and New York: Oxford University Press, 1987.

Rippin, Andrew. *The Qurān and Its Interpretive Tradition.* Variorum Collected Studies Series, CS715. Aldershot, Hampshire and Burlington, VT: Ashgate, 2001.

Schussman, Aviva. "The Prophet Ezekiel in Islamic Literature: Jewish Traces and Islamic Adaptations." In *Biblical Figures Outside the Bible*, edited by Michael E. Stone and Theodore A. Bergren, 316–39. Harrisburg PA: Trinity Press International, 1998.

Tottoli, Roberto. *Biblical Prophets in the Qur'an and Muslim Literature.* 1 edition. Routledge Studies in the Qur'an. London: Routledge, 2009.

Wheeler, Brannon M. *Moses in the Qur'an and Islamic Exegesis.* Routledge Studies in the Qur'an. New York: Routledge, 2002.

Fetal Positions

A bizarre—and in some ways, disturbing—premise of talmudic law states that a premature fetus in its seventh month might well be viable (the Talmud calculated that prophets like Isaac, Moses and Samuel were all seven-month births)—but an eight-month fetus has no chance whatsoever of surviving. This biological "fact" was so certain to the rabbis that they drew from it some very clear practical conclusions.

For example, although Jewish law, as is well known, always sets aside ritual prohibitions for the sake of saving human life, even if there is only a slight chance of doing so, it is nevertheless forbidden to violate the sabbath restrictions for the sake of an eight-month-term newborn, who is classified as a mere "stone"—and yet we *would* be required to override the sabbath laws for the sake of a seven-month fetus.

As odd as this belief might sound to us in light of modern biomedical science, it was by no means unusual in the ancient world. In fact, it was the prevalent view of the foremost Greek physicians; and it could have tangible legal repercussions for determining paternity or inheritances.

To Hippocrates were ascribed treatises on both "the Seven-Month Fetus" and "the Eight-Month Fetus." The author of those works accepted the doctrine about the non-viability of the eight-month fetus, but he did have some difficulty accounting for the anomaly. He tried to explain it in terms of a special malady that besets pregnant women during their eight month, a condition that enfeebles the child and places unusual pressures on the uterus and umbilical cord. However, fetuses that are born earlier or later than that time will not be endangered by the illness and therefore are likely to survive in a healthy state.

Galen, Avicenna and Hippocrates in a 16th-century medical book (from Bettmann Archive).

According to another theory shared by Greeks and Jews, there are in fact two separate classes of pregnancy, the seven-month and the nine-month kind. Either will produce a healthy child when they are carried to term. However, an unfortunate child who is born after eight months is probably a premature nine-monther who did not reach full term and is therefore not viable.

Several Greek writers theorized that the viability of seven-month fetuses should be credited to the special numerological status of the lucky number seven and its multiples (which distinguished it from the unlucky eight).

The polyglot Rabbi Abbahu, head of the talmudic academy of Caesarea, was once asked (evidently by some non-Jews, perhaps Christians) to provide a source for the distinction between the seven-month and the eight-month fetuses. He replied with an ingenious wordplay based on the numerological values of Greek letters. The letter "zeta" equals seven [hepta] while "eta" is "eight." These combine into a Greek sentence "zeta eta e ta hepta" that translates as: "Seven [i.e., a seven-month fetus] lives rather than eight."

Several of the authoritative codes of Jewish law, including Rabbi Joseph Caro's *Shulḥan 'Arukh*, accept the Talmud's position on eight-month fetuses without question.

However, some of the medieval Talmud commentators sensed that this did not dovetail with the observable facts. Rabbi Isaac of Dampierre was quoted in the Tosafot as ruling that nowadays it is permitted to handle any infant on the sabbath, since we do not possess sufficient expertise to determine the timing of the gestation, and therefore all births should be given the benefit of the doubt. Instead of measuring the viability with reference to chronological criteria, it is better to look at the physical signs of the child's development, such as the appearance of hair and nails, which are mentioned elsewhere in the Talmud as indicators.

A similar approach was favoured by Maimonides. He was, of course, an eminent medical practitioner, and he had no qualms when it came to ignoring or dismissing the more outdated medicinal prescriptions that he found in the Talmud. As it happens, his hero Aristotle was among the minority of Greek scientists who had challenged the factual basis of Hippocrates' theory. Nonetheless, in the present case Maimonides merely cited the pertinent talmudic rulings without expressing any doubts about their fundamental accuracy. Like Rabbi Isaac of Dampierre, he did recommend that the child's health be determined by observable physiological signs (hair and nails) and not by the imprecise practice of reckoning the length of the pregnancy.

As regards the practical implications related to the status of eight-month pregnancies, there has existed a virtual consensus among modern deciders of halakhah that such fetuses and newborns must be regarded as viable, and must be given access to any kind of suitable therapeutic treatment, including procedures that require violations of sabbath restrictions.

Rabbi Abraham Karelitz, the Ḥazon Ish

Nevertheless, this provokes a theological question that can be troubling to traditional believers: after all, there is unanimity in the medical community that the ancient perceptions concerning eight-month fetuses were just plain untrue. As long as the unborn child has reached a point of viability (a stage has become increasingly early thanks to advances in technology), then the closer it comes to the full nine-month term, the better are its chances for a safe and healthy birth. The eighth month is no exception to this pattern.

Indeed, there is a long tradition of respectable rabbis who have recognized that scientific pronouncements in the Talmud reflect the ideas of their times and need not be accepted with the same reverence that would be extended to the sages' religious teachings. In more recent generations, however, several Orthodox spokesmen have opted for more fundamentalist positions.

Rabbi Isaac Jacob Weiss

Some halakhists, like the twentieth-century authority Rabbi Isaac Jacob Weiss, sidestepped the theoretical issue, especially when discussing ritual implications that are not life-and-death issues (in his case, whether the widowed mother of a premature child should be considered "childless" for purposes of imposing the obligation of levirate marriage).

In a responsum devoted to the question, Rabbi Weiss stated that, notwithstanding consultations with a medical expert (who

סימן קכג

בענין ולד הנולד קודם זמנו שמבדיאים אותו באינקובטור.

שאלה. הנה בשו"ת אמרי יושר (ח"ב סי' קע"ז אות ב') נשאל. ע"ד המבואר בש"ע (אורח ס" ש"ל) דאם הפילה נפל שלא גמרו שערו וצפרניו. אין מחללין שבת עליו. עכשיו שנתחדש המכונה בפאריז ועוד עיירות גדולות. שאף נפל גמור. שלא גמרו שערו וצפרניו. מחממין אותו שם זמן גידולו וחי. מה יהי' הדין לענין שבת. וגם לענין חליצה. אחר שאיתמחי הרפואה עכ"ל.

כוונו. דמסתמא הנולדים באיפן זה כס חגשים מאד, כמ"ש בספר קם החיים (ש' שני"א חות כ') בשם ספר בית יהודה. וסה"ג כתב בספר זוכר הברית (סי' י' אות כ"ב). אף בענין נוכד במורש השביעי. ונא נגמרו שערו וספרניו. דפס נחשב בו שהיו בריא כשאר ונדיס. בליווף מה שגואיב שנא נגמרו ילורפו בשעיומה. אין נמוני עד שיתחזק ויבריא עיי"ש.

ג) והנה כפי המבואר בדברי הש"ם ופוסקים שם. ישנם ד' מיני וגדוח. ודאי כנו חדשיו. ודאי נא כנו חדשיו. ספק כנו חדשיו. וספחה וגדוח. וודאי כלו

The beginning of Rabbi Weiss's Responsum on the eight-month fetus

was also a religious Jew) who filled him in on the conventional scientific views, he preferred to accept the traditional talmudic theory, while noting the significance of recent technological developments. Thus, the essential fragility of eight-month fetuses remains a valid premise, but the introduction of sophisticated neonatal incubators now enables the survival of infants for whom no such possibility existed during the days of the Talmud.

A different approach was taken by Rabbi Abraham Karelitz, the "Ḥazon Ish," one of the most prominent spokesmen for Ḥaredi Judaism in Israel in the twentieth century. He acknowledged the glaring contradiction between present-day science and the statements of the rabbis of old. The only acceptable solution he could find to the conundrum was by resorting to a premise that had been employed by some earlier authorities—albeit very sparingly—to resolve similar discrepancies: he argued that since ancient times, humans have undergone an actual change in their physiological make-up that rendered the eight-month rule obsolete, even though it was perfectly valid in the days of the talmudic sages. It is hard to imagine that the Ḥazon Ish could really have been ignorant of the surviving forensic evidence in human anatomical remains from earlier times.

There is, to be sure, much to be said in the ongoing conversations between traditional religious texts, science and advances in medical technology. I suppose that it is all but inevitable that among the ranks of those who will make valuable contributions to that research, there will also be some scholars who entered the world as eight-month fetuses.

Bibliography:

Gutal, Neriah. *Sefer Hishtanut ha-Ṭṭeva'im ba-Halakhah: le-Verur Darkah shel Halakhah bi-Metsi'ut Mithalefet uve-Matsavim Mishtanim*. Jerusalem: Yaḥdav Institute, 1995.

Cohen, Dovid. "Shinuy Hateva: An Analysis of the Halachic Process." *Journal of Halacha and Contemporary Society* 31, no. 1 (1995): 38–61.

Hanson, Ann Ellis. "The Eight Months' Child and the Etiquette of Birth: 'Obsit Omen'!" *Bulletin of the History of Medicine* 61, no. 4 (1987): 589–602.

Klein, Michele. *A Time to Be Born: Customs and Folklore of Jewish Birth*. Philadelphia: Jewish Publication Society, 2000.

Lieberman, Saul. *Greek in Jewish Palestine: Studies in the Life and Manners of Jewish Palestine in the II-IV Centuries C. E.* New York: The Jewish Theological Seminary of America, 1942.

———. *Tosefta Ki-Feshuṭah*. Vol. 3 Mo'ed. New York: Jewish Theological Seminary of America, 1962. [Hebrew]

Neff, Estie. "Like a Stone: Scientific and Halakhic Solutions to the Eighth-Month Infant Phenomenon." *B'Or Ha'Torah* 23 (2014): 56–70.

Preuss, Julius. *Biblical and Talmudic Medicine*. Translated by Fred Rosner. Northvale, NJ: J. Aronson, 1993.

Reiss, Rosemary E., and Avner D. Ash. "The Eighth-Month Fetus: Classical Sources for a Modern Superstition." *Obstetrics & Gynecology* 71, no. 2 (1988): 270–73.

Roth, Pinchas. "Meir Ben Simeon Ha-Me'ili on Protracted Pregnancy." *Zutot: Perspectives on Jewish Culture* 13, no. 1 (2016): 11–25.

Steinberg, Avraham. *Encyclopedia of Jewish Medical Ethics*. Translated by Fred Rosner. Jerusalem and New York: Feldheim, 2003.

That Was No Lady, That Was My Allegory

Perhaps it is appropriate that the biblical book of Proverbs, ascribed to the wise king Solomon—whose wisdom had to compete with the demands of his seven hundred wives and three hundred concubines—should place a strong emphasis on advising its (presumably male) audience about the kinds of women that they should seek or avoid.

Traditional Jews will be most familiar with the *eshet ḥayil*, the "woman of valor"—that enterprising super-wife whose praises are the subject of the book's concluding chapter. (The epithet "*eshet ḥayil*" was appropriately adopted as the Israeli translation for the "Wonder Woman" television series, long before the role was given to Gal Gadot).

However, a perusal of the entire book of Proverbs will quickly reveal that its author was much more concerned with warning against the dangers that lurk behind the seductive temptations of certain ladies. One of the main benefits of wisdom lies in its ability "to deliver thee from the strange woman, even from the stranger which flattereth with her words."

Who exactly is this Strange Woman whose enticements are so hazardous to the reader's morals? I am inclined to read these passages as directed toward young men on the threshold of leaving the shelter of their homes to venture out into the big, scary world—essentially, admonishing the Dustin Hoffmans to avoid the sensuous clutches of the Anne Bancrofts. The woman in question is designated "strange" in the sense that she is forbidden to him. She is portrayed graphically as an adulterous cougar who prepares sensuous snares for the unwary y0uth while her husband is conveniently out of town.

This straightforward moralistic reading of the scriptural text was favoured by some commentators, ranging from Joseph ben Joseph ibn Naḥmias of fourteenth-century Toledo to the eighteenth-century Galician exegete Rabbi David Altschuler in his *"Meṣudat David"* commentary to Proverbs. Rabbi Abraham Ibn Ezra encapsulated the moral lessons to be derived from the context: "Just as wisdom can safeguard you from an evil man, so does it deliver you from women who are wicked and 'strange' by virtue of the fact that they have not mastered virtuous behaviour, so that it is *as if* they were of foreign birth."

On the other hand, the foremost traditional Jewish exegete, Rashi, was positively indignant at the suggestion that a book devoted to the theme of wisdom should squander its holy words to convey such a trivial lesson, arbitrarily singling out one particular sin from among the many that should be eschewed by righteous followers of the Torah. He therefore insisted that the Strange Woman must be understood as a metaphoric allusion to a more fundamental religious offense, that of heresy. From Rashi's rabbinic perspective, the gravest threat to a Jew would consist of "rejecting the yoke of the commandments"; and the wording of his interpretation strongly implies that he has in mind the Christian church and its antipathy toward literal observance of the Law.

This would have been consistent with a tradition that appears in the Talmud's tale about Rabbi Eliezer ben Hyrcanos who was once favourably impressed by a homiletical interpretation that he had heard from a certain Jacob of Kefar-Sekaniah, a follower of Jesus of Nazareth. Later, Rabbi Eliezer was himself arrested for his alleged involvement with the illicit sect. He accepted his predicament as a deserved retribution for his commendation of Christianity. This experience prompted him to cite the passage from Proverbs about the Strange Woman: "Remove thy way far from her," which he applied to heresy. It would appear that Rashi's dissatisfaction with a literal interpretation of the Strange Woman had been felt by some of the earliest known readers of the book of Proverbs.

Thus, unlike other volumes of the ancient Greek biblical translation, which are generally quite literal, the Proverbs translation included in the "Septuagint" takes extensive liberties and reformulates key phrases, so that it is speaking not about the erotically beguiling woman of the Hebrew text, but about a more abstract threat: "O son, let not *evil counsel* overtake you, which has abandoned the teaching of youth and forgotten the divine covenant." It is this "evil counsel," rather than a seductive woman, that will lead the unwary to the grave.

A widely accepted scholarly thesis has it that the author of this translation, a member of the Hellenized Jewish community of ancient Alexandria, transformed the scriptural image of the alluring lady into a metaphor for Greek philosophy, the most conspicuous and attractive form of foreign wisdom that was threatening to tempt Jews away from their tradition. In keeping with the familiar biblical imagery, the translator equated such intellectual enticements with an

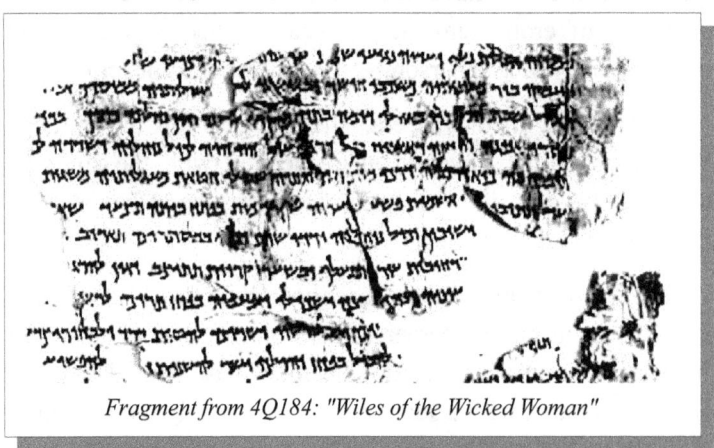
Fragment from 4Q184: "Wiles of the Wicked Woman"

adulterous betrayal of Israel's marriage-covenant with the Almighty—an attitude that was uncannily similar to the one that would be voiced by Rashi more than a thousand years later.

The imagery of the evil temptress also dominated an intriguing document from the Dead Sea Scrolls, a work that bears the official name "4Q184" but which is usually referred to by the more descriptive title "Wiles of the Wicked Woman." Insofar as we may reconstruct from the fragmentary remains of that ancient scroll, it appears that the woman is demonic in her insidious wickedness. Evidently, she resides in the midst of the eternal flames of the underworld from which she emerges to lure the unwary to their spiritual doom by batting her lovely eyelashes. Amid all this vivid imagery, it is not entirely clear what the metaphor was intended to represent. Numerous theories have been proposed to interpret her as a depiction of erotic temptation, sectarian heresy, theological unbelief, or even as a personification of the corrupt Jerusalem.

During the medieval era, the imagery of the Strange Woman was often invoked in connection with the study of philosophy—and it was used both by the advocates of rationalism and by its opponents.

The German-born Rabbi Asher ben Jehiel (the "Rosh") was invited late in his his career to take on the leadership of the Jewish community in Toledo, Spain, where he had his first close encounters with a Judaism that was deeply committed to philosophy and secular learning, including the application of rationalism and science to the derivation of religious law.

The Rosh was adamant in his resistance to such approaches, insisting that those who relied on scientific reasoning rather than on traditional talmudic argumentation threatened to undermine the very foundations of Jewish religious authority. In support of his position he argued, "It is regarding this that the wise man says 'None that go unto her return again'." Like a man who has been corrupted by a voluptuous woman, a scholar who has been initiated into scientific methods will never again be able to return to the ways of authentic rabbinic discourse, "because his mind will always be focused on natural science and he will constantly be inclined to make comparisons between the two disciplines... This will ultimately result in perversions of justice because the two are in reality mutually opposed and rivals that cannot coexist."

But have no fear. The Jewish philosophers were also perfectly capable of utilizing the Strange Woman image in support of their own doctrines. Maimonides explained the motif as an allegory for the Aristotelian concept of metaphysical Form that gives rational structure to chaotic Matter; and by extension, the need for the structured human intellect to maintain control over the the unruly (and presumably feminine) imaginative faculty.

Similarly, in accordance with the psychological theories of his age, Gersonides portrayed the relationship between the seductress and her male prey as a symbol for the "'appetitive soul" that was believed to house the physical urges within every person and conspires to lure the rational mind away from its proper intellectual goals, though such desires are alien and foreign to essential human nature: "She entices him, drawing him to rebelliousness and sin by means of her beauty when his imaginative faculty causes him to perceive reprehensible actions as pleasant."

Whether one chooses to apply the image of the Strange Woman to foreign philosophies, to undisciplined imaginations and desires, or to any other alien force that threatens their spiritual integrity—it is still advisable for callow youths to exercise some caution when lured by actual enchantresses who might lead them into indiscretions or heartbreak.

Bibliography:

Alfonso, Esperanza. "Late Medieval Readings of the Strange Woman in Proverbs." In *Medieval Exegesis and Religious Difference: Commentary, Conflict, and Community in the Premodern Mediterranean*, edited by Ryan Szpiech, First edition., 187–99. Bordering Religions: Concepts, Conflicts, and Conversations. New York: Fordham University Press, 2015.

Allegro, John M. "Wiles of the Wicked Woman: A Sapiential Work from Qumran's Fourth Cave." *Palestine Exploration Quarterly* 96 (1964): 53–55.

Aubin, Melissa. "'She Is the Beginning of All the Ways of Perversity:' Femininity and Metaphor in 4Q184." *Women in Judaism* 2, no. 2 (2001): 1–23.

Baumgarten, Joseph M. "On the Nature of the Seductress in 4Q184." *Revue de Qumran* 15, no. 1–2 (1991): 133–43.

Kraus, Wolfgang, Michaël N. van der Meer, Martin Meiser, and Seth A. Bledsoe, eds. "'Strange' Interpretations in LXX Proverbs." In *XV Congress of the International Organization for Septuagint and Cognate Studies: Munich, 2013*, 6781–694. Society of Biblical Literature, 2016.

Cook, Johann. " 'Išāh Zārāh (Proverbs 1-9 Septuagint): A Metaphor for Foreign Wisdom?" *Zeitschrift Für Die Alttestamentliche Wissenschaft* 106, no. 3 (1994): 458–76.

———. *The Septuagint of Proverbs: Jewish And/Or Hellenistic Proverbs?: Concerning the Hellenistic Colouring of LXX Proverbs*. Brill, 1997.

Distefano, Michel G. *Inner-Midrashic Introductions and Their Influence on Introductions to Medieval Rabbinic Bible Commentaries*. Studia Judaica 46. Berlin and New York: Walter de Gruyter, 2009.

Fox, Michael V. "The Strange Woman in Septuagint Proverbs." *Journal of Northwest Semitic Languages* 22, no. 2 (1996): 31–44.

Gazov-Ginzberg, Anatole M. "Double Meaning in a Qumran Work (The Wiles of the Wicked Woman)." *Revue de Qumran* 6, no. 2 (September): 279–85.

Geyser-Fouché, Ananda. "Another Look at the Identity of the 'Wicked Woman' in 4q184." *HTS Teologiese Studies / Theological Studies* 72, no. 4 (November 30, 2016): 9 pages.

Goff, Matthew. "Hellish Females: The Strange Woman of Septuagint Proverbs and 4QWiles of the Wicked Woman (4Q184)." *Journal for the Study of Judaism* 39, no. 1 (January 1, 2008): 20–45.

Hengel, Martin. *Judaism and Hellenism: Studies in Their Encounter in Palestine During the Early Hellenistic Period.* 2 vols. Philadelphia: Fortress Press, 1981.

Irsai, O. "Ya'akov of Kefar Niburaia—A Sage turned Apostate." *Jerusalem Studies in Jewish Thought* 2, no. 2 (1982): 153–68. [Hebrew]

Loader, William R G. "The Strange Woman in Proverbs, Lxx Proverbs and Aseneth." In *Septuagint and Reception: Essays Prepared for the Association for the Study of the Septuagint in South Africa*, 209–27. Leiden: Brill, 2009.

Melamed, Abraham. "Maimonides on Women: Formless Matter or Potential Prophet?" In *Perspectives on Jewish Thought and Mysticism*, edited by Alfred L. Ivry, Elliot R. Wolfson, and Allan Arkush, 99–134. Amsterdam: Harwood Academic Publishers, 1998.

Moore, Rick D. "Personification of the Seduction of Evil: 'The Wiles of the Wicked Woman.'" *Revue de Qumran* 10, no. 4 (1981): 505–19.

Schäfer, Peter. *Jesus in the Talmud.* Princeton, N.J: Princeton University Press, 2007.

Tigchelaar, Eibert J. C. "The Poetry of the Wiles of the Wicked Woman (4q184)." *Revue de Qumran* 25, no. 4 (2012): 621–33.

Wright, Benjamin G. "Wisdom and Women at Qumran." *Dead Sea Discoveries* 11, no. 2 (2004): 240–61.

Saint Gamaliel

There are not many talmudic rabbis who have been canonized as Christian saints. The only one that I know of who merited that dubious distinction was Rabban Gamaliel the Elder. The Orthodox church honours him on August 2 of their liturgical calendar, and the Roman Catholics on the following day.

Rabban Gamaliel lived during the last years of the Second Jewish Commonwealth and was a respected spokesman for the Jewish sect of Pharisees who evolved, after the destruction of the second Temple, into the Rabbis of the Talmud and Midrash. We know much less about him and his teachings than about his grandson, the Rabban Gamaliel who was active in the rabbinic academy of Yavneh in the generation following the Temple's destruction.

The attitudes of the early Christian church towards the Pharisees, as reflected in the various works included in their New Testament, were not uniform. Jesus and Paul accepted Pharisaic doctrines like the belief in bodily resurrection. A passage in the Gospel of Matthew has Jesus advising his followers to follow the Pharisaic teachings because "the scribes and the Pharisees sit in Moses' seat"—though he goes on at greater length to warn against emulating their behaviour, which he characterized as arrogant, ostentatious and hypocritical.

Rabban Gamaliel: from the Sarajevo illuminated Haggadah

In fact, the few explicit references to the Pharisees in rabbinic literature are not very different in their tone from the New Testament passages, depicting them as people who made ostentatious demonstrations of their piety, and were so narrowly focussed on petty matters of ritual and propriety that they lost sight of the larger moral issues.

And yet the Pharisee elder Gamaliel received a much more sympathetic treatment in Christian tradition. This descendant of the illustrious Hillel the Elder was himself an acknowledged scholar and religious leader, and his name was invoked in two passages in the New Testament's "Acts of the Apostles."

When Paul of Tarsus was called before the council of Jesus's followers in Jerusalem to account for his negative assertions about the Torah and for his welcoming of unconverted gentiles into the church (which at this stage saw itself as a strictly Jewish movement), he proudly presented his credentials as one who was "brought up in this city at the feet of Gamaliel, and taught according to the perfect manner of the law of the fathers."

Furthermore, when the Sadducees and priests were demanding the prosecution of Peter and other followers of Jesus, it was the Pharisee Gamaliel, "a teacher of the law held in respect by all the people," who made a reasoned argument against an excessive response. He cited precedents from other failed messianic resistance movements, those of Theudas and Judah of Galilee, that had been allowed to follow their own ambitions without interference—only to be ultimately crushed by the Romans. Presumably the same fate would befall these followers of the current messiah if left to their own devices. Gamaliel concluded his argument: "And now I say to you, keep away from these men and let them alone; for if this plan or this work is of human origin, it will come to nothing."

The text in the New Testament includes an additional inference that I suspect was inserted by the Christian editor: "but if it is of God, you cannot overthrow it, lest you even be found to fight against God." In recent years, this approach, referred to as "the Gamaliel principle," has been invoked by many Christians as a practical guideline that mandates a passive wait-and-see attitude when reacting to potential heresies or rival religions.

Gamaliel's reasoning was accepted by the priestly assembly and they released the Christians with an admonition to refrain from further missionary activity. The author is quick to note that they happily ignored those instructions and resumed their energetic preaching.

Gamaliel's presence in the New Testament meant that he also made appearances in several cinematic biblical epics, where his role has been played by capable actors like John Houseman and José Ferrer.

The traditions about Rabban Gamaliel seem to reflect the situation that prevailed during the early evolution of the Jewish "Jesus movement" before it consolidated into a separate religion that stood in opposition to a mainstream rabbinic Judaism. As the lines separating the respective communities became more clearly demarcated, both of them tended to inhabit ideological enclaves that were clearly polarized between "us" (the virtuous followers of the true religion) and "them" (the wicked heretics or deceivers).

This created something of a dilemma for Christians who had to find a place for that sympathetic Pharisaic sage, Gamaliel. By then, the only way for a person to get onto the list of "good guys" was by becoming a Christian. The fourth-century church father John Chrysostom outlined Gamaliel's problematic status: "One may well wonder, how, being so right-minded in his judgment, and withal learned in the law, he did not yet believe. But it cannot be that he should have continued in unbelief to the end." The only plausible solution to this impasse was to conclude that Rabban Gamaliel did indeed convert to Christianity!

Gamaliel appearing to St. Lucian: detail from alter-piece by Hans Klocker (15th century)

An ancient "historical novel" known as the "Recognitions of Clement" took the form of an imaginary memoir by a companion of the apostle Peter. It included an expanded, dramatic retelling of the confrontation between Gamaliel and the priests. In that version, however, we find an additional detail: Gamaliel "was secretly our brother in the faith, but by our advice he remained among them." That is to say, the wise Pharisaic sage had converted to Christianity, but kept the conversion under wraps so that he could serve as an undercover "mole" on behalf of his new community. And in fact, he made good use of his strategic position in order to alert his new allies about any impending schemes to harm them.

This motif invites comparison with a tradition that was current in some medieval Jewish biographies of Jesus [the genre known as "*Toledot Yeshu*"] according to which Jesus's most prominent disciples were actually loyal Jews, but in order to protect their people they chose to establish Christianity as a foreign religion, with separate Latin scriptures, in order to divert the wrath of the Roman authorities away from the Jewish nation. To be sure, midrashic tradition also had a tendency to turn virtuous gentiles, such as Jethro, Rahab, or the Roman ruler "Antoninus" (who was an amicable companion of Rabbi Judah the Patriarch) into converts to Judaism.

In the late sixth century, the Presbyter Eustratios of Constantinople was able to add that both Gamaliel and his otherwise unknown son named Abib had been baptized by the apostles Peter and John. It was reported of several Christian holy men that Gamaliel appeared to them in dreams to inform them where they might find his remains along with the relics of other martyrs, thereby allowing them to be reinterred in a church in Constantinople in 428. One of those visionaries described the Jewish sage as "a tall, venerable man with a long white beard. He was dressed in white clothing which was edged with gold and marked with crosses, and held a gold wand in his hand."

That might not be a distinctive enough image to brand him as a competitor to Santa Claus or a super hero—but one never knows if some enterprising greeting-card company will seize the opportunity to resuscitate the tradition of celebrating St. Gamaliel's Day.

Bibliography:

Alon, Gedalia. *The Jews in Their Land in the Talmudic Age, 70-640 C.E.* Translated by Gershon Levi. Jerusalem: Magnes Press, 1980.

Bauckham, Richard. "Gamaliel and Paul." In *Earliest Christianity within the Boundaries of Judaism: Essays in Honor of Bruce Chilton*, edited by Alan Avery-Peck, Craig A. Evans, and Jacob Neusner, 87–106. The Brill Reference Library of Judaism 49. Leiden and Boston: Brill, 2016.

Chilton, Bruce D., and Jacob Neusner. "Paul and Gamaliel." *Bulletin for Biblical Research* 14, no. 1 (2004): 1–43.

Crabbe, Kylie. "Being Found Fighting Against God: Luke's Gamaliel and Josephus on Human Responses to Divine Providence." *Zeitschrift Für Die Neutestamentliche Wissenschaft* 106, no. 1 (2015): 21–39.

Falk, Harvey. *Jesus the Pharisee: A New Look at the Jewishness of Jesus*. Wipf and Stock Publishers, 2003.

Flusser, David. "Gamaliel, the Teacher of the Law." *El Olivo: Documentación Y Estudios Para El Diálogo Entre Judíos Y Cristianos* 6, no. 15 (1982): 41.

Lyons, William John. "The Words of Gamaliel (Acts 5.38-39) and the Irony of Indeterminacy." *Journal for the Study of the New Testament* 20, no. 68 (1998): 23–49.

Neusner, Jacob. *The Rabbinic Traditions about the Pharisees before 70*. Leiden: Brill, 1971.

Schürer, Emil. "IV. Major Torah Scholars." In *A History of the Jewish People in the Time of Jesus*, edited by Géza Vermès, Fergus Millar, and Martin Goodman, 2:356–80. London, New Delhi, New York, Sydney: Bloomsbury T. & T. Clark, 2014.

Wright, N. T. *Paul and the Faithfulness of God*. Christian Origins and the Question of God 4. London: Society for Promoting Christian Knowledge, 2013.

The Poem on the Pedestal

It is hardly surprising that on August 2 2017, when U. S. administration spokesman Stephen Miller tried to defend President Trump's policies of restricting refugees and immigrants, the first reaction of the press was to contrast that mean-spirited attitude with the words of welcome etched onto the pedestal of the Statue of Liberty

> Give me your tired, your poor,
>
> Your huddled masses yearning to breathe free,
>
> The wretched refuse of your teeming shore."

Somewhat more surprising was Mr. Miller's retort, to the effect that the poem in question was a later addition and not integral to the original statue. I'm not certain how relevant that point was to the issue at hand—but it does happen to be true.

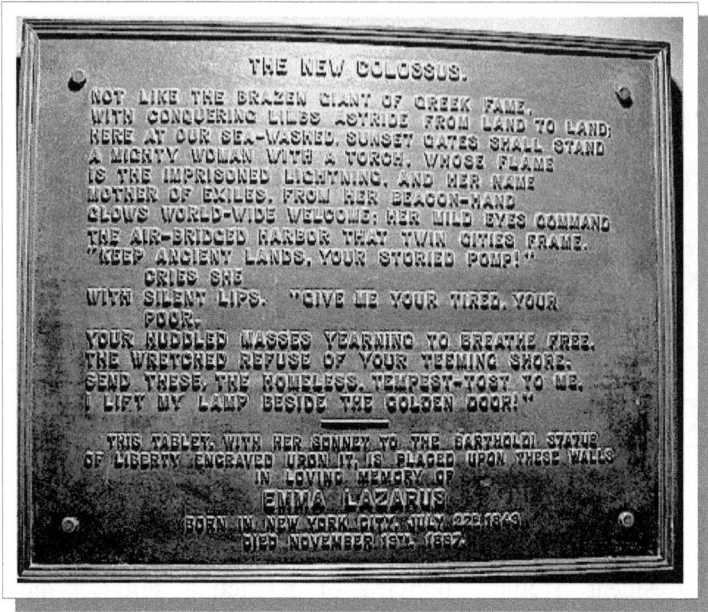

Another fact that was not given conspicuous emphasis in the discussions was the Jewish identity of the poem's author, Emma Lazarus (1849-1887). She was the scion of Jewish families that been in America since pre-Revolutionary times; her mother's lineage from Germany and her father's of Sephardic origin. The Lazarus family proudly identified as Jews and were active members of New York's venerable Congregation Shearith Israel Spanish and Portuguese synagogue, though Emma claimed to find little that was personally relevant in the traditional rituals and liturgies of her ancestral religion.

Indeed, the complicated relationships between Lazarus, her sonnet, her Judaism and the statue make for a fascinating story.

Emma Lazarus was an acclaimed poet with ambitions of finally putting American literature on the international map. She belonged to the most prominent literary milieus in America and abroad and was respected by the likes of Turgenev, Browning and Henry James.

As is well known, the Statue of Liberty was a gift to America from the people of France—well, not exactly. For one thing, its original name was not really the "Statue of Liberty," but rather "La Liberté éclairant le monde" (Liberty enlightening the world), with its implied sentiment that Liberté is a supremely French spécialité (if one ignores such minor detours as the Reign of Terror or the Napoleonic empire) that is being generously shared with the less enlightened folk of the world.

And then there was the matter of the statue being a gift—that was not entirely accurate either. The French authorities insisted that the pedestal be provided and paid for by the recipients. It was in this respect that Emma Lazarus came to be involved in the project. The inclusion of her poem "the New Colossus" on the pedestal was expected to serve as a lucrative attraction for potential donors in a fund-raising drive to pay for the pedestal.

The statue project had originally been formulated in 1865 by the French statesman and jurist Edouard de Laboulaye who hoped that it would somehow inspire the French themselves to fulfill their highest ideals.

The lady whose likeness is represented is the Roman goddess Libertas. The sculptor, Frédéric Auguste Bartholdi, also had in mind another image from classical mythology, namely the Colossus of Rhodes, that huge representation of the sun-god that was counted among the Seven Wonders of the ancient world. Bartholdi derived especial satisfaction from the fact that his bronze creation would be larger than the original Colossus. In the popular consciousness, the Statue of Liberty did come to be associated with the Colossus, and that association lies at the root of Lazarus's consenting to adorn the statue with a poem called "the New Colossus."

When she was first approached in late 1883 about providing a poem that could be auctioned off for the "Bartholdi Pedestal Fund," Lazarus would have nothing to do with it. After all, she was not some commercial jingle-writer who could produce masterpieces on demand; and in any case she had little sympathy for the triumphalist grandeur that was embodied in the enormous brazen image. A recent visit to Europe had left her profoundly underwhelmed by the debris of French ideologies.

What ultimately persuaded her to take on the task was when her recruiter, the author Constance Harrison (who sometimes wrote under the name "Refugitta"), presented it to her as a personal challenge: it would give her an opportunity to subvert the statue's purpose in ways that represented her own version of authentic American values.

In the end, this subversive goal was what defined the true theme of her famous sonnet. The lady with the torch in New York harbour was "*not* like the brazen giant of Greek fame, / With conquering limbs astride from land to land." As stated in her poem (which contains no mention of the statue's original French ideal of "Liberty"), America is not stirred by colossal grandeur or pompous professions of abstract ideals. Instead, it honours the caring "Mother of Exiles" who compassionately welcomes the "huddled masses yearning to breathe free."

Emma Lazarus

It would appear that Emma Lazarus's vision of an America that embraced wretched masses of destitute foreigners was as controversial then as it is now. There were plenty of reasons for oppressed and starving Europeans to be fleeing to the shores of the New World—but Emma Lazarus felt a particular closeness to the plight of the Jews who were escaping from Czarist Russia and European anti-semitism in what was beginning to emerge as one of the most massive waves of migration in modern history. (Among those migrants would be the Jewish forebears of White House spokesman Stephen Miller who were fleeing from Belarus). Lazarus's personal encounters with Jews who suffered dreadful persecution also inspired her to recommend (prior to the emergence of the political Zionist movement) the creation of a haven for oppressed Jews in their historic homeland.

Like several other genteel Jewish ladies of her generation, Emma took a personal role in visiting and assisting the new arrivals; and she made use of her literary skills and political connections to plead on their behalf against those who were either indifferent to their suffering or ideologically committed to a narrower definition of who should be counted as "real" Americans. The early 1880s witnessed the enactment of the first American legislation defining various kinds of undesirables who were to be filtered out by means of a bureaucracy newly created for the purpose.

There has hardly been a single discussion about immigration policy in which the Lazarus sonnet has not been cited; including, for instance, the 1996 episode of the Simpsons in which Police Chief Wiggum began to enforce Springfield's new immigration restrictions: "Here's the order of deportations. First we'll be rounding up your tired, then your poor, then your huddled masses yearning to breathe free…"

Lazarus's "New Colossus" poem contains no explicitly Jewish references. The only detail that might be interpreted as a Jewish image is the epithet "Mother of Exiles," which is reminiscent of Jeremiah's poignant depiction of the matriarch Rachel "weeping for her children refusing to be comforted." This should not be misconstrued as an indication that the author was ignorant of or indifferent to Hebrew tradition. Quite the contrary—her oeuvre is replete with poems on Jewish topics, not only about the familiar biblical themes that are part of western civilization's shared heritage, but also about figures who were of distinctively Jewish relevance, such as Bar Kokhba, Rashi, Judah Halevi and Ibn Gabirol. She was an avid student of Jewish history and literature, and a considerable portion of her published work is devoted to translations (usually *via* German) of Hebrew literary classics. Her interest in Jewish culture tended to gain intensity when provoked by persecution, anti-semitism or the appropriation of noble Jewish values by Christians.

Bibliography:

Cavitch, Max. "Emma Lazarus and the Golem of Liberty." *American Literary History* 18, no. 1 (2006): 1–28.

Eiselein, Gregory, ed. *Emma Lazarus: Selected Poems and Other Writings*. Broadview Literary Texts. Peterborough, ON and Orchard Park, NY: Broadview Press, 2002.

Kessner, Carole S. "From Parnassus to Mount Zion: The Journey of Emma Lazarus, on the Centenary of Her Death." *Jewish Book Annual* 44 (1987): 141–62.

Marom, Daniel. "Who Is the 'Mother of Exiles'? Jewish Aspects of Emma Lazarus's 'The New Colossus.'" *Prooftexts* 23, no. 3 (2000): 231–61.

Trachtenberg, Marvin. *The Statue of Liberty*. New York: Viking, 1976.

Turner, Chris. *Planet Simpson: How a Cartoon Masterpiece Defined a Generation*. 1st Da Capo Press ed. Cambridge, MA: Da Capo Press, 2004.

Vogel, Dan. *Emma Lazarus*. Twayne's United States Authors Series 353. Boston: Twayne Publishers, 1980.

Wagenknecht, Edward. "Emma Lazarus: 1849-1887." In *Daughters of the Covenant: Portraits of Six Jewish Women*, 23–54. Amherst: University of Massachusetts Press, 1983.

Wolosky, Shira. "An American-Jewish Typology: Emma Lazarus and the Figure of Christ." *Prooftexts* 16, no. 2 (1996): 113–25.

Young, Bette Roth. "Emma Lazarus and Her Jewish Problem." *American Jewish History* 84, no. 4 (1996): 291–313.

———. *Emma Lazarus In Her World: Life and Letters*. Philadelphia: Jewish Publication Society of America, 1995.

Arriving at Ararat

When listening to the musical "Hamilton" I am struck by how acutely aware its protagonists were that they were participating in an exciting new political experiment that would allow them to change the world in revolutionary ways.

There was at least one prominent Jewish figure among the circles who shared in that adventure. Mordecai Manuel Noah (1785-1851) of Philadelphia made a name for himself as a journalist, playwright, civil servant and politician. In 1814 he was appointed to the post of American consul to Tunisia where he successfully resolved a notorious case involving an American fishing boat that was captured and enslaved by Barbary pirates.

President Monroe soon dismissed him from his post. Monroe admitted that Noah's religion was the reason for his removal—but that his motives were not anti-semitic. Rather, he feared that it would create diplomatic obstacles when negotiating with Muslims (though in those days Jews usually had an an advantage over Christians in such situations); and in any case, the consul had overspent his budget for ransoming the crew, a charge for which he was subsequently exonerated.

Mordecai Manuel Noah

Noah warned that the United States should be careful not to erode the support of the Jews at home or abroad. He claimed that European Jewry constituted a commercial network of sufficient influence that it was in the American interest to maintain their good will.

On the other hand, he was also well aware that the Old World could be a very hostile and dangerous place for Jews, and therefore the welcoming tolerance of America could play a momentous role in shaping the national destiny of the people of Israel. He articulated his extraordinary vision in an address before the Shearith Israel congregation in 1818: "Until the Jews can recover their ancient rights and dominions and take their ranks among the governments of the earth, this is their chosen country; here they can rest with the persecuted of every line, secure in person and property, protected from tyranny and oppression and participating of equal rights and immunities."

There you have it. Noah never abandoned the traditional Jewish expectation that the national sovereignty to which they are entitled would one day be restored in their historic homeland. In the meantime, however (as Theodor Herzl would later decide when offered an interim solution in Uganda) there was a pressing need for a temporary haven in which Jews could be accepted and protected as equals—and that haven was the pioneering experiment in universal civil rights: America.

Noah's project enjoyed support from Christians whose eschatological theologies called for a restoration of Jewish sovereignty (many of them believed this would lead to their conversion to the True Faith) as a precondition for Christ's return in the Millennium.

The collapse of the Ottoman empire seemed to confirm this scenario, as did certain features of the European Enlightenment. Although generally indifferent or hostile to nationalism and religious parochialism, Napoleon had recently made a flamboyant show of convening Europe's Jewish religious leaders in the framework of a revived Sanhedrin, Israel's ancient supreme court. Noah, who maintained ties with Abbé Henri Gregoire, the outspoken French champion of liberal ideals and inter-faith brotherhood, undoubtedly regarded such a development as a harbinger of imminent redemption in the new liberal world order.

But Mordecai Manuel Noah's vision of the Jewish future in America was not limited to a passive confidence in his country's receptiveness to Jewish refugees, nor in the Jewish readiness to assume the responsibilities of productive citizenship. He took it upon himself to found a Jewish state within the United States of America: the colony of Ararat to be established on Grand Island in the Niagara River near Buffalo, New York, not far from the Canadian border. He argued that settling the area with Jews would help guard the region from Canadian encroachment.

It is nigh impossible to find a description of the founding ceremony for the Ararat project that manages to keep a straight face or avoid sarcasm when outlining the flamboyant pomposity that Noah brought to Buffalo, which was then little more than a sleepy rural village of about 2,500. Contemporary observers were dubious as to whether there were significant numbers of Jews in attendance. At any rate, the area of Grand Island could not have accommodated more than a few dozen families—though there are indications that he expected the pilot project to be further expanded after its initial success. For the occasion, Noah got hold of whatever he could find with an impressive or gaudy uniform–including parades of Masons, military companies, an Indian Chief, exotically costumed musicians and volleys of cannons. Noah himself wore a colourful costume borrowed from a production of Richard III, and made his entrance to the strains of the "Conquering Hero" theme from Handel's Judas Maccabeus. Numerous biblical texts were incorporated into the ceremony. On the nascent city's cornerstone were engraved the words of the "Sh'ma Yisra'el."

The cornerstone of Noah's proposed Ararat colony, now in the Buffalo Town Hall

The official proclamation of Ararat took place in the town's largest edifice, St. Paul's Episcopal church. To Noah's enumeration of his various professional and political credentials he added "and by the grace of God, Governor and Judge of Israel." He went on to proclaim "to the Jews throughout the world that an asylum is prepared and offered to them, where they can enjoy the peace, comfort and happiness which have been denied them through the intolerance and misgovernment of former ages." In other speeches he spelled out in detail how the current venture would serve as a watershed in the sad trajectory of Israelite history since biblical times. To be sure, the Judaism practiced here would be of a particularly enlightened variety. In particular, he declared that polygamy would be abolished (this had been a major concern at Napoleon's "Sanhedrin"); and that Ararat would be receptive to Hebrews of all varieties, including such exotic flavours as Karaites, Samaritans, those from India and Africa —and especially to the native Americans who, in keeping with the widespread belief of the time, were remnants of Israel's "ten lost tribes" (Noah himself composed a tract on the subject). Although Noah believed that safety from persecution might be achieved by means of assimilation, he found that option unacceptable. Jews should strive to proudly cultivate their heritage and Hebrew language. Emulating ancient Jewish practices and anticipating the methods later adopted by the Zionist movement, he called for a three-shekel "capitation tax" to be levied upon all the Jews of the world to defray the new state's expenses. He made efforts to recruit Jews in Europe, though not all his advertisements reached their intended addresses.

The name "Ararat" was of course a clever pun on Noah's own surname, and it evoked the image of an ark full of Jewish refugees being rescued from a European deluge. He also made use of other biblical expressions, notably that of "cities of refuge" originally devised as a place to which perpetrators of involuntary manslaughter could escape harm from their victims' avengers.

The ambitious project elicited more than its share of ridicule, parody and insinuations that it might be nothing more than a clever real estate scam. There is no evidence of a single Jew, including Noah himself, ever setting foot on the Grand Island colony.

Though Ararat may have been a failure, it could be argued that the entire continent ultimately came to fulfil Noah's original vision. More than two million Jews were able to escape the hardships and perils of central and eastern Europe before the gates were closed under the Immigration Restriction Act of 1924. Those refugees and their children were thereby saved from the clutches of European tyrants and murderers, in numbers that could never have squeezed into Mordecai Noah's little refuge on the Niagara River.

Bibliography:

Cone, G. Herbert. "New Matter Relating to Mordecai M. Noah." *Publications of the American Jewish Historical Society* 11 (1903): 131–37.

Gelber, Natan M. "Mordecai Emanuel Noah: His Dream of a Jewish State in America." *Sura* 3 (1958 1957): 377–413.

Goldberg, Isaac. *Major Noah: American-Jewish Pioneer.* Freeport, NY: Books for Libraries Press, 1972.

Gordis, Robert. "Mordecai Manuel Noah: A Centenary Evaluation." *Publications of the American Jewish Historical Society* 41 (1951): 1–28.

Kohn, S. Joshua. "Mordecai Manuel Noah's Ararat Project and the Missionaries." *American Jewish Historical Quarterly* 55, no. 2 (1965): 162–96.

Popkin, Richard H. "Mordecai Noah, the Abbé Grégoire and the Paris Sanhedrin." *Modern Judaism* 2, no. 2 (1982): 131–48.

Rock, Howard B. *Haven of Liberty: New York Jews in the New World, 1654-1865.* Vol. 1. 3 vols. City of Promises: A History of the Jews of New York. New York: New York University Press, 2013.

Rovner, Adam. *In the Shadow of Zion: Promised Lands Before Israel.* New York and London: NYU Press, 2014.

Sarna, Jonathan D. *Jacksonian Jew: The Two Worlds of Mordecai Noah.* New York: Holmes & Meier, 1981.

Shalev, Eran. *American Zion: The Old Testament as a Political Text from the Revolution to the Civil War.* New Haven: Yale University Press, 2013.

———. "Revive, Re-New and Reestablish: Mordecai Noah's Ararat and the Limits of Biblical Imagination in the Early American Republic." *American Jewish Archives Journal* 62, no. 1 (2010): 1–20.

Weingrad, Michael. "Messiah, American Style: Mordecai Manuel Noah and the American Refuge." *AJS Review* 31, no. 1 (2007): 75–108. doi:10.2307/27564261.

Weinryb, Bernard D. "Noah's Ararat Jewish State in Its Historical Setting." *Publications of the American Jewish Historical Society* 43 (1953): 170–91.

The Time of Our Life

In his pioneering theological treatise "The Book of Doctrines and Opinions," the tenth-century scholar Saadiah Gaon devoted a brief but significant discussion to the question of whether there is a set length to a person's lifespan. As was his wont, he formulated his inquiry in terms of biblical texts. On the one hand, Scripture contains passages such as the divine blessing that "the number of thy days I will fulfill" that imply that a person is assigned a predetermined number of days. On the other hand, however, texts such as "the fear of the Lord prolongeth days, but the years of the wicked shall be shortened" seem to teach that your spiritual or moral stature can have a decisive impact on how long you live.

A central text for many Jewish discussions of this question is the Bible's story of king Hezekiah who was informed by the prophet Isaiah that his death was imminent—and yet the king's contrite prayers succeeded in prevailing upon the Almighty to add fifteen more years to his life.

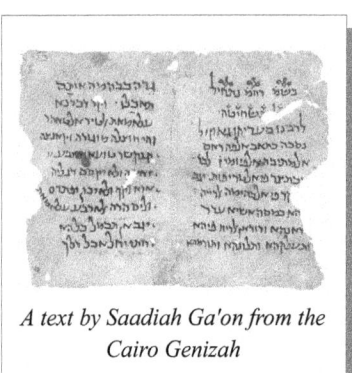

A text by Saadiah Ga'on from the Cairo Genizah

Saadiah argued that the Almighty assigns to each of us a default lifespan that corresponds to the basic physical health of the body into which one is born. This is usually around seventy years in keeping with the words of the Psalmist that "the days of our years are threescore years and ten." This lifespan, however, is by no means immutable. Indeed, it is within a person's power to extend it by as much as thirty years or to shorten it, depending on lifestyle choices and other factors—including the inscrutable dictates of divine will and wisdom.

In discussing the question, Saadiah observed that it would make no sense to believe that lifespans are entirely unalterable and that everybody dies on a predetermined date. If that were the case, there would be no sense to those many tales in the Bible in which God or his agents smite the wicked through violence, plagues or other means; or where the righteous are rewarded with longevity.

Rav Hai Gaon also devoted one of his responsa to this question and its implications. His chief concern was with the concept of divine foreknowledge; specifically: how was God able to "know" the mutually contradictory facts about the times of Hezekiah's promised and actual demise. Hai proposed a subtle logical differentiation between this case of God's knowing what will occur the future, as distinct from the death being a fulfillment of the divine foreknowledge.

Hai Gaon discussed in considerable detail the thesis that if everyone dies at their predetermined time, then no guilt can be assigned to a murderer who happens to be the physical agent of the death. This question was also addressed by Maimonides in a responsum cited by a medieval commentator. The great philosopher was responding to a query from his disciple Joseph ben Judah Ibn Simeon: "Is the length of a person's life set to a particular time, which the person will necessarily reach, so that it cannot be abbreviated or cut short? Or alternatively, are harmful circumstances capable of shortening a person's lifespan when they affect a person who has failed to take appropriate precautions?"

Now, the answer to this question strikes us as quite straightforward—so straightforward, in fact, that it is hard to understand why the foremost philosophical minds in the Jewish world felt impelled to deal so seriously with the obvious truism that lifespans are subject to variation.

For a better understanding of the importance of this question, we must look to the Muslim intellectual environment in which Saadiah, Hai and Maimonides were all writing.

In the Qur'an, it is possible to point both to passages that assert that the length of a mortal life is inexorably predetermined, as well as to texts declaring that our lives are entirely subject to divine control. Alongside a statement such as "when their designated time has come, they cannot put it off by a single hour, nor can they advance it," there are also also passages that speak of God's striking down sinners before their time.

The concept of a pre-set length to people's lives was known in Arabic as *"ajal,"* and it generated much discussion among Islamic scholars. Whereas Jews typically tended to avoid making dogmatic pronouncements on theological questions, Islamic authorities such as the influential theologian al-Ash'ari formulated an official position that reinforced the subordination of humans to divine decrees.

This was consistent with the broader Muslim approach to the questions of free will and determinism, regarding which the definers of orthodoxy usually opted for a fatalistic or passive outlook in which puny mortals are powerless against divine omnipotence. The political leaders of the early Muslim community, especially the Umayyad Caliphs, sometimes promoted this deterministic philosophy as a way of justifying the reigns of rulers whose religious or ethical standards were less than perfect. If this premise were followed to its logical conclusion, then a leader who seized power by assassination had not necessarily committed a sin, since the victim was destined to die at that time anyway. We have seen above that Hai Gaon discussed precisely this case. Saadiah too speculated about whether such a hypothetical plea might be used in order to exonerate Jezebel for her massacre of the prophets.

This fatalistic outlook on life and death may well have contributed over the ages to a reluctance in Muslim societies to protest or rebel against vicious and bloodthirsty tyrants. Indeed, the earliest school of rational theology in Islam, known as the Mu'tazila, originated as a movement of protest against corrupt leadership. One of the movement's cardinal tenets was that people cannot be subjected to the final divine judgment unless they possess free will. Accordingly Mu'tazilites discoursed at length about the relationship between *ajal* and divine foreknowledge, as well as whether violent deaths fulfill the *ajal* or undermine it.

As a rationalist and a scientist, Maimonides had little patience for the theological hair-splitting of his Muslim and Jewish predecessors, especially when they claimed to have intimate understanding of the workings of divine wisdom. For Maimonides, God is essentially unknowable, and it is presumptuous to imagine that we can analyze his reasoning. Instead, he approached the question from more pragmatic directions—from the perspective of the Torah, as well as from a scientific or medical standpoint.

As regards the Torah, Maimonides cited a selection of biblical precepts that involve taking realistic precautions to ward off life-threatening dangers. These include the requirement to erect railings on rooftops; the institution of cities of refuge to protect unintentional killers from acts of vengeance; or the military exemptions granted to newlyweds and others to keep them from falling in battle.

Like Saadiah, Maimonides cited verses that invoked length of days as a reward for righteousness and obedience to God. He also agreed with Saadiah in declaring that there is no automatic correlation between righteousness and longevity.

As regards the scientific aspects of the question, Maimonides drew upon his thorough expertise in medical lore to provide a systematic listing of circumstances that, if not averted, might lead to fatal results. These range from the removal or destruction of vital organs to sudden shocks of joy or fear, which allegedly do their damage by altering the delicate balance of body heat. Reckless conduct (such as refusal to inoculate against potential illnesses) can bring on an early demise—but by choosing a cautious and sensible lifestyle, it is possible to steer clear of most of those threats and to live a long life.

That kind of prudent advice is unquestionably timeless.

Bibliography:

Brody, Robert. *Sa'adyah Gaon*. Oxford and Portland, OR: The Littman Library of Jewish Civilization, 2013.

Griffel, Frank. *Al-Ghazālī's Philosophical Theology*. Oxford University Press, 2009.

Hafeez, Abdul. "The Antinomy of Free Will and the Appointed Term (Ajal Musamma)." *Hamdard Islamicus* 23, no. 4 (2000): 63-68.

Maimonides, Moses. *Teshuvat HaRaMBa"M BiShe'elat HaKeṣ HaKaṣuv LeḤayyim*. Edited by Gotthold Weil and Michael Schwartz. Tel-Aviv: Papyrus Publishing House, 1979. [Hebrew]

———. *Über Die Lebensdauer*. Edited by Gotthold Weil. Basel: Karger, 1953.

Weil, Gotthold. "Teshuvato Shel Rav Hai Ga'on 'al ha-Keṣ ha-Kaṣuv la-Ḥayyim." In *Sefer Asaf: Koveṣ Ma'amare Meḥkar Mugash li-Khvod ha-Rav Prof. Śimḥah Asaf 'al-yede Yedidav Ḥaverav ve-Talmidav liMlot Lo Shishim Shanah*, edited by Umberto Cassuto, 261-279. Jerusalem: Mossad Harav Kook, 1953. [Hebrew]

Wolfson, Harry Austryn. *The Philosophy of the Kalam*. Harvard University Press, 1976.

A Preacher's Dream and an Artist's Vision

I suppose that this is the ultimate dream of every rabbi and preacher. At the conclusion of the service, the congregants emerge from the sanctuary with nothing in their minds but the images of the scriptural reading and the sermon that they have just heard. So lasting and vivid was that spiritual experience that they actually believe that they are seeing it reenacted before their eyes as they walk outside.

Precisely such a scene was the subject of a famous painting by Paul Gauguin in 1888 titled "Vision after the Sermon: Jacob Wrestling with the Angel." The picture portrays a group of peasant women who are standing outside a church observing the scene of Jacob struggling with the angel, as described in the book of Genesis.

The creation of this work marked a turning point in Gauguin's artistic development—and apparently in his spiritual evolution as well.

Now the main outlines of the artist's life are well-known. Product of a respectable bourgeois upbringing, he was educated in prestigious Catholic schools and pursued careers in the merchant marine and navy and in finance. His success as a stockbroker was abruptly cut short in 1882 with the crash of the Paris stock market, and he found that he now had nothing to lose by devoting himself to his true passion for art. He joined the circles of the Impressionists, sharing some of their interest in the techniques of portraying light and in landscape painting. Eventually, however, his fascination with the "primitive" impelled him to travel to the West Indies and, more significantly, to Tahiti where his most memorable works were produced.

But in 1888, Gauguin and many of his fellow painters were gravitating toward the lovely rural vistas of northern France which offered them unparalleled opportunities to study nature and the effects of natural light. Gauguin's "Vision after the Sermon" was created at Pont-Aven in Brittany; however, it is glaringly clear that it bears little resemblance to the kind of output that we expect from the Impressionists. If anything, it is reminiscent of a panel from a comic-strip, rendered in two-dimensional shapes in unrealistic primary colours. As it happens, this style, known as "Cloisonnism," was inspired by the techniques exemplified by the Japanese artists Hiroshige and Hokusai that were enjoying popularity in France at the time.

Paul Gauguin, "Vision after the Sermon" National Gallery of Scotland, Edinburgh

More significant, to my mind, was Gauguin's selection of subject matter. Apparently he chose to paint these ladies as they were stirred by their experience at prayer because they provided him with the best available instance of vital religious life within the range of localities accessible to him. Like many educated post-enlightenment Frenchmen, and in spite of (or as some have suggested: *because* of) his lackluster Catholic schooling, Gauguin had little personal sympathy for things religious, and he tended to associate faith with primitive, premodern culture. The nearest remnant he found to old-time religious faith was among the simple peasantry of the Brétagne countryside.

This premise is one that was solidly entrenched in the academic study of religions. It was common for scholars to seek after an "essence" of religion which they often equated with the original, primordial spirituality from which all the subsequent manifestations of faith and ritual had evolved (a concept that had some kinship with the notion of the "noble savage"). This hypothetical essence could supposedly be reconstructed from the features common to the developed religions, but remnants of it were also to be found in the "savage" cultures that continue to exist outside the bounds of western civilization.

Gauguin, Self-portrait, Orsay Museum

It might have been the quest for these undiluted vestiges of human spirituality that eventually drew Gauguin to the pristine Eden of the South Seas—but at this point in his life he felt that the most approachable version of primitive religion was to be discerned among the peasantry of northern France. In one of his letters, the artist expressed his personal pride that he had "painted a religious picture, very clumsily but it interested me and I like it." He boasted of his achievement in evoking a mood of severity and the characters' "great rustic and superstitious simplicity."

In the picture, the visual area assigned to the Breton women (which he referred to as the "natural" area) is separated from the ("non-natural") scene of the biblical drama by a diagonal tree-trunk which Gauguin (in a letter to his friend Vincent van Gogh) identified as an apple tree. It is widely assumed that this symbolized the "tree of knowledge of good and evil" in the garden of Eden which in European translations is usually identified as an apple tree, and which somehow functions here as the border line between day-to-day existence and spiritual vision.

Of all the biblical scenarios and sermon topics that Gauguin might have selected for his painting, why did he choose the particular episode of Jacob's wrestling match? Judaism has generally read that story in connection with Israel's struggle over the inheritance of the divine blessing. However, interpreters who are trying to grasp its significance for Gauguin's inner life point out correctly that in Christian tradition the contest is usually read as a metaphor for people's internal struggles with our consciences or our sinful natures.

In the painting, the group of those who behold Jacob's struggle consists of twelve peasant women all of them wearing the traditional helmet-like white bonnets. There is also a sole tonsured priest or monk who might be intended as a self-portrait of the artist. Of course the number twelve is a meaningful one for Jacob, as it represents the number of his sons who became the twelve tribes of Israel. However, it is more likely that the allusion here is to Jesus' twelve apostles who were charged with spreading his "good news" to the world.

One puzzling component of the picture is a cow that is situated in the space between the ladies and the tree. Although its placement in the physical zone (rather than in the segment assigned to the biblical vision) would suggest that it is to be perceived as part of the physical landscape rather than a symbol, this fact has not discouraged art critics from speculations about its supposed spiritual meaning, particularly through its association with redemptive sacrifice, a theme that likely dated back to the region's pre-Christian Celtic heritage that was later endowed with Christian overtones.

At any rate, the primary factor that most probably impelled Gauguin to portray the scene of Jacob and the angel was because it happened to be the actual "*parashah*" that formed the theme of the sermon, as part of the church service on the particular days in August when he painted his masterpiece. This was in accordance with the venerable local practice of the Celtic Church (which diverged from the mainstream Roman Catholic liturgical calendar).

More specifically, a nearby chapel in the village of Pluméliau was dedicated to St. Nicodème who was revered locally as a protector of flocks, herds and horned animals. A special rite of blessing the animals was part of his celebration (known as a "Pardon") in August, as were Sunday-afternoon wrestling competitions in which young men vied to impress prospective brides. After all, a successful sermon should serve as a conduit between the ancient scriptural texts and the specific realities of the congregation.

It is a telling indication of Gauguin's genius that more than a century later spectators are still striving to grapple with the significance of his artistic vision. This kind of creative achievement provides sublime gratification for teachers, authors—and preachers—when their students and readers persist in wrestling with their ideas and values.

Bibliography:

Andersen, Wayne V., and Barbara Klein. *Gauguin's Paradise Lost*. New York: Viking Press, 1971.

Brettell, Richard R. *The Art of Paul Gauguin*. Washington: National Gallery of Art, 1988.

Coignard, Jérôme. "La Vision après le Sermon." *Connaissance des Arts*, no. 757 (2017): 84–87.

Facos, Michelle. *An Introduction to Nineteenth Century Art*. New York: Routledge, 2011.

Fraser, Donald Hamilton. *Donald Hamilton Fraser on Gauguin's Vision After the Sermon—Jacob Struggling with the Angel*. Painters on Painting. London: Cassell, 1969.

Herban III, Mathew. "The Origin of Paul Gauguin's Vision after the Sermon: Jacob Wrestling with the Angel (1888)." *The Art Bulletin* 59, no. 3 (1977): 415–20.

Maurer, Naomi E. *The Pursuit of Spiritual Wisdom: The Thought and Art of Vincent Van Gogh and Paul Gauguin*. Madison and London: Fairleigh Dickinson University Press and Associated University Presses in association with the Minneapolis Institute of Arts, 1998.

Powers, Edward D. "From Eternity to Here: Paul Gauguin and the Word Made Flesh." *Oxford Art Journal* 25, no. 2 (2002): 89–106.

Silverman, Debora. *Van Gogh and Gauguin: The Search for Sacred Art*. 1st ed. New York: Farrar Straus and Giroux, 2000.

Thomson, Belinda, Frances Fowle, and Lesley Stevenson. *Gauguin's Vision*. Edinburgh: National Galleries of Scotland, 2005.

Cagney, Kelly...and a Coin Clattering in a Keg

I recently had occasion to watch the 1941 film "Strawberry Blonde" on television. It takes place in New York during the 1890s and tells the story of scrappy young Biff (James Cagney) who is struggling to rise above his lowly economic situation, but in the meantime is distracted by the lovely but shallow Virginia (Betty Grable, the blonde of the title) who eventually ditches him.

At that point the Cagney character becomes appreciative of the more genuine qualities of Amy (Olivia De Havilland). His conservative temperament had previously been put off by her posturing as a "free-thinker" whose mother had been a Bloomer Girl, her aunt an actress and she herself a cigarette smoker! Nevertheless Biff is now impelled to make an aggressive pass at her. Tearfully, Amy now owns up that she is really an innocent girl and her background was not really quite as scandalous as she had presented it. Mother had merely expressed admiration for the Bloomer Girls (but Father had forbidden her to act on it), Auntie's theatrical experience had been confined to church productions, and her own cigarettes were never lit.

To this revelation Cagney retorts: "Just as they say: 'An empty barrel makes the most noise.'"

The film never bothers to divulge the identities of "they," and it seems to assume that the average moviegoer will understand the point of the proverb.

My own reaction, as someone who is familiar with Jewish traditional literature, was along the lines of "Hey, Jimmy Cagney just quoted from the Talmud!"

The passage I had in mind appears in the Babylonian Talmud in the context of an exposition of a verse from the biblical book of Proverbs: "Wisdom resteth in the heart of him that hath understanding: but that which is in the midst of fools is made known."

By way of illustrating the contrast between wisdom that rests unobtrusively inside one's heart and the kind which is broadcast publicly, Rav Ḥama applied the former text to a student who is the heir to a family of Torah scholars; whereas the latter speaks of a scholar who comes from an uneducated background, so that his wisdom stands out in sharp contrast to the ignorance of the rest of his family environment.

The Talmud then introduces a comment by the sage 'Ulla: "It is as they say: An *istira* in a *lagin* calls: kish, kish."

This proverb might benefit from a few explanations. The Aramaic "istira" alludes to the Greek "stater," a widely circulated denomination of (usually) silver coinage in the ancient Mediterranean world. The "lagin" was a medium-sized ceramic or glass vessel that was often kept in the dining room, especially at formal dinners, and used to fill cups with wine after the beverage had been removed from its original storage barrel. 'Kish kish" is the onomatopoeic sound of a coin rattling against the insides of an otherwise empty container.

As the commentators understood it, 'Ulla's proverb was being attached to Rav Ḥama's distinction between pupils from scholarly and ignorant families, in order to exemplify how a scholar appears much more conspicuous against a background of uneducated kinsfolk. I prefer to attach it directly to the biblical text, which is being understood as saying that inferior intellects always make a point of actively publicizing their thoughts however banal they might be—and therefore there is an inverse proportionality between people's boastful oratory and their actual intelligence.

A seventeenth-century Yiddish lexicon of proverbs and folk sayings, the *Mar'eh Mussar* (*Tzucht-Shpigl, Mirror of Morals*) by Seligman Ulma-Guenzburg of Hanau, proposed some alternative ways of expressing this idea: "A half-penny coin in an empty money-box jingles much more than if it contained a thousand gold coins," or: "At first he talks big but then does nothing—a lot of wind to no avail."

Entry "Istira Balagina" in Ulma-Guenzburg's "Mar'eh Mussar"

In any case, 'Ulla's analogy is to of a solitary coin clattering about and making the "kish kish" noise in an otherwise empty container. If the same object had been deposited inside a purse that was packed with coins, the sound would have been muffled and inaudible. This fits quite nicely with the context of Jimmy Cagney's line in the movie, which conveys the meaning of: "I never took your boasting seriously, since everybody knows that the louder the clatter the less basis it has in fact."

Did the creators of "Strawberry Blonde" know the Talmudic passage? Unlikely, but not altogether unimaginable. The authors of the screenplay's final version were the prominent team of Julius and Philip Epstein, a pair of twins who were responsible for such masterpieces as "Casablanca" "Arsenic and Old Lace." Although the Epstein brothers were Jewish, their pre-university education took place in the New York City public school system and they do not appear to have received any substantial Jewish instruction.

If "they" (the source of Cagney's adage) were not the rabbis of the Talmud, then who were they? The next likely suspect in such cases is often Shakespeare—and our present search there does in fact produce a positive result. In some of the plays in the bard's historical cycle there appears a character named Ancient (or: Ensign) Pistol, one of Falstaff's cronies and a drinking buddy of Prince Hal's dissolute youth, who eventually enlists in the French campaign that is the subject of "Henry V." This swaggering, sycophantic loudmouth comes across as a cowardly and opportunistic braggart who is constantly inflating his negligible accomplishments. One character says of him, "I did never know so full a voice issue from so empty a heart. But the saying is true: 'The empty vessel makes the greatest sound.'"

A similar idea is voiced by the loyal Earl of Kent in "King Lear" when he tries without success to persuade his misguided monarch that Cordelia's understated filial affection is more authentic than the ostentatious fawning of her elder sisters: "Thy youngest daughter does not love thee least, nor are those empty-hearted whose low sound reverbs no hollowness."

There are a few earlier instances of proverbs that make a similar point. One of my favourites appears in an essay by Plutarch, an ancient writer whose observations often dovetail with those of his contemporary rabbis. The premise of his essay "Concerning Talkativeness" (De Garrulitate) is that garrulous talkers are usually very poor listeners and therefore miss out on much of what they should be hearing. "Consequently, while others retain what is said, in talkative persons it goes right through in a flux; then they go about like empty vessels, void of sense, but full of noise."

Now let's fast-forward to October 2017 when White House Chief of Staff Gen. John Kelly, accused (inaccurately, it seems) Florida's Democratic Congresswoman Frederica Wilson of taking credit for something she had not done. Gen. Kelly placed her "in a long tradition of empty barrels making the most noise."

In a retort that puzzled even the administration's most ardent opponents, the African-American Wilson insisted that "empty barrel" was...a racist expression! For a few days the American news media were scrambling to track down reasons why the expression or its background could by any stretch of the imagination carry racist connotations. As far as I can tell, the best they could come up with was the claim that any criticism of a black woman by a privileged white male must be stigmatized as racist and sexist.

Advocates of liberal education have often looked back nostalgically to the days when civilized society was held together by its partaking in a shared cultural and literary heritage, so that people could assume that their listeners would recognize and understand allusions to the Bible or Shakespeare (and perhaps even an occasional quote from the Talmud). Whatever the weaknesses of that shared heritage (yes, it is overwhelmingly European and male), it probably is preferable to our present situation of incoherent discourse among virtual illiterates who are thereby stunted in their abilities to communicate meaningfully.

But that's just my own two cents. Hopefully they are not just rattling around in an empty pot.

Bibliography:

Brand, Yehoshua. *Ceramics in Talmudic Literature*. Jerusalem: Mossad Harav Kook, 1953. [Hebrew]

Epstein, Julius J., and Philip G. Epstein. *The Strawberry Blonde (1941): Shooting Script*. Alexandria VA: Alexander Street Press and Warner Brothers, 1941.

Munro, Lucy. "Speaking History Linguistic Memory and the Usable Past in the Early Modern History Play." *Huntington Library Quarterly* 76, no. 4 (2013): 519–40.

Shmeruk, Chone. *Yiddish literature in Poland: Historical Studies and Perspectives*. Jerusalem: The Magnes Press, the Hebrew University, 1981.

Sokoloff, Michael. *A Dictionary of Jewish Babylonian Aramaic of the Talmudic and Geonic Periods*. Ramat-Gan and Baltimore: Bar Ilan University Press and Johns Hopkins University Press, 2002.

Sperber, Daniel. *Roman Palestine, 200-400, Money and Prices*. 2nd ed. with supplement. Bar-Ilan Studies in Near Eastern Languages and Culture. Ramat-Gan: Bar-Ilan University Press, 1991.

Steinschneider, Moritz. "Jüdisch-deutsche Literatur, nach einem handschriftlichen Katalog der Oppenheim'schen Bibliothek (in Oxford)." *Serapeum* 10 (1849): 9–16.

Yeck, Joanne L. "Epstein, Julius and Philip." In *International Dictionary of Films and Filmmakers*, edited by Sara Pendergast and Tom Pendergast, 4th ed., Vol. 4: Writers and Production Artists:267–69. Detroit: St. James Press, 2000.

Zevulun, Uzza, and Yael Olnick. *Function and Design in the Talmudic Period*. Tel-Aviv: Haaretz Museum, 1978. [Hebrew]

Vital Organs

Traditional Jewish theology affirms the belief in an omniscient deity. As formulated in Maimonides' thirteen articles of faith, the creator "knows all the deeds of human beings and all their thoughts."

In the idiom of biblical Hebrew, one of the most common ways to express the idea that God has access to our innermost thoughts and desires is by means of expressions like Jeremiah's "I the Lord search the heart, I test the kidneys."

Those readers who are more familiar with the classic King James English version might be better acquainted with the wording "I try the reins." That, however, is not an allusion (figurative or otherwise) to the straps that are used to restrain a horse, but is rather an obsolete synonym for the kidney, derived from the Latin "renes," the same root that gives us English derivatives like "renal," and even "adrenalin."

The premise that underlies those expressions is that the kidney, like the heart, is a locus of thought, emotion and especially moral judgment—a conception that may have originated in ancient Egypt. Of course, scientific physiology has long since reassigned those mental functions to the brain, which did not figure very prominently in that capacity in ancient literatures; although it is the cardiac blood-pump that continues to provide the favourite metaphors for love in valentine cards, bumper stickers and emojis.

Perhaps it is possible to write off those scriptural phrases as nothing more than convenient examples of interior parts of the human anatomy, an approach that was indeed favoured by Rabbi Abraham Ibn Ezra. The rabbis of the Talmud, however, were clearly of the opinion that the expressions were to be understood with literal precision. In a passage that enumerates the functions of the various human organs, no distinction is made between biological, mental or emotional functions, and the power of counsel is ascribed to the kidneys. A midrashic homily speculates that Abraham, who had no access to human teachers in his heathen environment, must have learned the Torah from the wisdom that was housed in his own kidneys.

More specifically, the Talmud taught: "A person possesses two kidneys. One of them advises him for good and one advises him for evil. It stands to reason that the good one is on one's right side and the evil one on the left, as it is written, 'A wise man's heart is at his right hand; but a fool's heart at his left.'" I like to imagine them as those little figures of a halo-topped angel and a pitchfork-wielding devil who argue out moral decisions in cartoons.

Most rabbinical scholars in the medieval Sephardic and Italian realms received a thorough medical or philosophical training; so it would eventually come to their attention that the prevailing scientific theories did not support the traditional Hebrew understanding of the kidneys' functions.

As a rule, discrepancies of this sort did not provoke severe theological dilemmas among the faithful. After all, Maimonides had long since declared that the scientific pronouncements of the ancient rabbis should not necessarily be accepted dogmatically, since they were not essential parts of the received Torah tradition, but merely reflected the sages' personal opinions or the scientific theories that were current in their environment. However, this solution could not be easily invoked for the kidney question, since its earliest source was not in the Talmud or Midrash, but in the Bible itself. We therefore find that several rabbis had to make special efforts to uphold the claim that the kidneys are a source of human thought and counsel.

This problem became particularly acute in Renaissance Italy. New experimental methods in medical research were overthrowing the long-entrenched systems of Aristotle and Galen.

Vital Organs

Rabbi Moses Provençal of Mantua (1503–1576) was asked how to reconcile the rabbinic statements about the kidney with the tenets of contemporary physicians and biologists who spoke of the brain as the centre of intellect and judgment. In his responsum, the rabbi submitted that in this case the teaching of the Jewish sages is to be preferred. To be sure, the scientists may be forgiven for getting it wrong; after all, unlike the sages of Israel, they do not enjoy the benefits of an unbroken chain of tradition that extends back via the biblical prophets and elders to the divine revelation at Mount Sinai.

Discussion about kidneys in Lampronti's Paḥad Yiṣḥak

In a very similar vein, his contemporary Rabbi Isaac Lampronti observed that even though the achievements of medical science might appear very impressive to us, their work is of necessity limited to observable phenomena; but as long as they are unable to grasp every aspect of the innumerable details that constitute reality, they will not have truly penetrated into the deeper meanings of the processes they are describing. As regards the specific topic of human biology, the secular scientists do not fully understand the systems of nourishment and growth, or the sources of bodily strength and vigor.

Rabbi Lampronti therefore viewed the purely empirical knowledge of the scientists as essentially superficial, to be contrasted with the profound wisdom of the Jewish sages who were privy to the divine secret of creation. "Anyone who is intimately familiar with it will be capable of achieving wonders that are far more numerous than what the scientists can boast—wonders that they can accomplish by means of the science of alchemy or through natural magic."

Rabbi Lampronti noted that of all the internal organs, the kidneys are the only ones that come in pairs. This ties in neatly with the Talmud's statement about how they serve to advise the lone heart to pursue either virtuous or sinful options. The Talmud's linking of the two kidneys with the good and evil inclinations supports those interpreters who regard the kidneys' impact as rooted in sexual desire—which can take the form either of participation in wholesome family life or of destructive promiscuity.

On further reflection, the linking of thoughts and moods with internal physical organs does not strike me as inherently irrational. True, for centuries western thinking was dominated by the doctrine of "Cartesian dualism" (named for French philosopher René Descartes) and its conviction that the human mind is an abstract entity that is essentially independent of the physical body that houses it. However, traditional religious thought, especially the kind that found expression in medieval Jewish moralistic writings, maintained a more nuanced approach, observing that the health or illness of one's body can exert a powerful influence on a person's intellectual abilities. Rationalists like Maimonides insisted that we must follow a strict moral discipline in order to rein in biological urges that are constantly tempting us away from our spiritual or intellectual missions.

Current medical science is more cognizant of how human behaviour can be influenced by the activities of various glands, hormones or drugs that are secreted or processed by internal organs. While there is no evident indication that the kidneys are counted among the organs that affect our reasoning, there was no prima facie reason for pre-moderns to rule such ideas out of hand.

Judah Halevi touched on this matter briefly in his *Kuzari*, arguing that the relationship between the kidneys and human intelligence is analogous to the impact of physiological masculinity on men's cognitive functions. In a definitive expression of chauvinism and political incorrectness, Halevi did not make reference, as a modern writer would likely have done, to testosterone-inspired belligerence or violence, but rather to the indisputable fact (according to the science of his time) that eunuchs are observably less intelligent—even when compared to creatures of limited intellectual capacity, such as... women (who also happen to be incapable of growing beards)!

Somehow I have a gut feeling (on the right side, of course) advising me that I should not accept such views unquestioningly.

Bibliography:

Diamandopoulos, Athanasios, Andreas Skarpelos, and Georgios Tsiros. "The Use of the Kidneys in Secular and Ritual Practices According to Ancient Greek and Byzantine Texts." *Kidney International* 68, no. 1 (2005): 399–404.

Ruderman, David B. "Contemporary Science and Jewish Law in the Eyes of Isaac Lampronti of Ferrara and Some of His Contemporaries." *Jewish History* 6, no. 1–2 (1992): 211–24.

———. *Jewish Thought and Scientific Discovery in Early Modern Europe*. New Haven: Yale University Press, 1995.

Langermann, Y. Tzvi. "Science and the 'Kuzari.'" *Science in Context* 10, no. 3 (1997): 495–522.

Leibowitz, Yeshayahu, Daniel Kahneman, and Yoram Yovel. *Mind and Brain: Fundamentals of the Psycho-Physical Problem*. Edited by Yoram Yovel. Sidrat Heksherim. Jerusalem: The Van Leer Jerusalem Institute and Hakibbutz Hameuchad, 2005.

Maio, Giovanni. "The Metaphorical and Mythical Use of the Kidney in Antiquity." *American Journal of Nephrology* 19, no. 2 (1999): 101–6.

Preuss, Julius. *Biblical and Talmudic Medicine*. Translated by Fred Rosner. Northvale, NJ: J. Aronson, 1993.

Slifkin, Natan. "The Question of the Kidneys' Counsel." Rationalist Judaism, 2010.

Wake-Up Call

Let's face it. For many of us getting out of bed in the morning can be a challenging ordeal.

It is therefore understandable that the traditional Jewish morning prayers begin with a series of blessings (texts following the formula "blessed are you, Lord God...") that address the arduous process of waking up.

Most of those blessings stem from a passage in the Talmud in which each one is attached to a specific stage in the process: opening one's eyes, sitting up, standing straight, getting dressed and so forth. Early in the Middle Ages, the Babylonian Ge'onim instituted the practice of reciting them all sequentially as part of the synagogue ritual.

As is the case with many Jewish blessings, it is not always easy to distinguish between the ones whose purpose is to endow an action with the status of a religious precept, to express our gratitude, or to convey the praises of the Almighty.

Amidst all this liturgical richness there is one particular blessing, at the end of the list, that many of us find most germane to our physical and mental states when the alarm clock—or, as the Talmud presumes, the crowing of the rooster — rouses us from our slumbers: "Blessed are you, Lord God, sovereign of the universe, who gives strength to the weary." Indeed, sometimes I have the feeling that without a bit of supernatural nudging I would be incapable of overcoming my grogginess, returning to consciousness and setting about my morning regimen.

The first recorded discussion of this blessing was by Rabbi Jacob ben Asher in his code of Jewish law, the "*Arba'ah Ṭurim.*" Rabbi Jacob's comments are of particular interest because, though he composed his code in Toledo, Spain, he was actually born in Germany from which he migrated in 1303, and he was thus acutely conscious of the variations in custom and legal traditions between the main centers of Jewish culture. In his enumeration of the obligatory passages to be included in the early morning service, he observed, "There is an additional blessing included in the Ashkenazic prayer books: 'Blessed are you... who gives strength to the weary.' It was ordained because a person entrusts his soul at night into the hands of the Holy One when it is weary from labouring hard all day, but he restores it to him in the morning in a rested and peaceful state."

Rabbi Jacob's interpretation was inspired by a parable from the midrashic compendium Genesis Rabbah: Citing a text from the book of Lamentation, "renewed each morning, great is your trustworthiness," Rabbi Simeon bar Abba expounded: "By virtue of how you renew us each and every morning, we know how great is your trustworthiness to restore the dead to life!" That is to say, the fact that last night's worn and weary body can wake up refreshed and invigorated is a marvel that is comparable to the resurrection of the dead in the messianic future. On many mornings I can personally sympathize with that impression. Some later commentators read the blessing as a reassurance to the nation of Israel that they will be restored to vitality after the lethargy of exile.

The religious sentiment underlying the blessing seems beyond reproach. Nevertheless, there was considerable resistance to incorporating it into the standardized liturgy. The main objection was that it did not have a source in the Talmud—even though the expression itself comes from the Bible where it was uttered by Isaiah: "He giveth power to the faint, and to them that have no might he increaseth strength."

As Rabbi Jacob ben Asher observed, the recitation of the blessing was initially confined to the realm of Ashkenazic Jewry. It makes its earliest known appearance in a manuscript of the Ashkenazi prayer book that was written in the twelfth century. Though it achieved some currency in French and

German communities, even in those localities there were authorities who tried to keep it out of their prayer rites on the premise that all Jewish practice must be strictly and exclusively governed by the Talmud—a principle that had been laid down by Rabbi Jacob ben Asher's own father, Rabbi Asher ben Jehiel. For that reason Rabbi Joel Sirkes (died 1640) would later suggest that the blessing would not have been adopted unless it had been found in earlier versions of the Talmud text.

In the sixteenth century, Rabbi Joseph Caro's *Shulḥan Arukh* upheld the conservative attitude that opposed any tampering with the authoritative sources of tradition; even though he was sympathetic to Rabbi Jacob's appealing rationale for reciting the blessing. This would normally have ended the discussion, at least among the Sephardic communities for whom Caro's *Shulḥan Arukh* was the definitive arbiter of Jewish law. On the other hand, the glosses of Rabbi Moses Isserles, which supplemented Caro's rulings with alternative traditions developed in the Ashkenazic schools, concluded that "the widespread custom among the Ashkenazim is to recite it." This in fact was something of an overstatement, as the practice had never came close to being a uniform policy.

Rabbi Caro himself completed his law code in the holy land, and he spent the latter years of his life as a prominent leader of the intensely kabbalistic community of Safed in the Galilee. Like most previous rabbis who followed the teachings of Kabbalah, he was generally quite resolute about not allowing mystical texts (such as the Zohar) to impinge on the integrity of the halakhic decision-making process. However, with the ascendancy of Rabbi Isaac Luria and his mystical circle, Kabbalah was making increasing claims to constituting an autonomous legal authority.

Although Luria himself did not commit his mystical teachings or his liturgical customs to writing, his disciples reported that he had taken issue with Caro's ruling and insisted that the blessing "who gives strength to the weary" ought to be recited in the morning rites. As befits mystical thinkers, the reason that was given for the blessing was a profoundly metaphysical one emanating from the kabbalistic doctrine of reincarnation. The human soul earns spiritual "garments" that are woven for it in proportion to each person's performance of meritorious deeds. In a manner reminiscent of Indian Karma, these garments accompany the soul through its various incarnations. This motif appears to have entered Jewish lore via a tale in Rabbi Nissim ben Jacob Ibn Shahin's eleventh-century anthology of inspirational tales, which derived in turn from an Arabic source.

As explained by Luria's most important interpreter Rabbi Haim Vital, at bedtime the righteous entrust their souls to the celestial powers for overnight "laundering"—whereas the sinners who are still lacking any spiritual garments are provided with brand-new ones. "A person who possesses a garment, but is weary, is supported and given strength."

According to this scenario, the blessing about giving strength to the weary is linked with the one in praise of the Lord "who clothes the naked" that was recited when dressing oneself in the morning. When both of the blessings are understood in their allegorical senses, the distinction comes to hinge on whether the soul in question is being issued a new garment or is having their existing one refurbished. From the kabbalistic perspective, the uttering of prayers does not merely express one's adherence to a spiritual attitude or theological belief, but actually has the power to alter spiritual reality.

This is bringing us into some very complicated and strenuous intellectual territory. It might be advisable to take a break, and to revisit the subject in the morning, after being refreshed by a good night's sleep.

Bibliography:

Baneth, D. H. "'Haluqa de-Rabbanan,' 'Hibbur Yafeh Min Ha-Yeshu'ah' and a Mohammedan Tradition." *Tarbiz* 25, no. 3 (1956): 331–36. [Hebrew]

Benayahu, Meir. "Rabbi Ḥayyim Viṭal bi-Yrushalayim." In *Yerushalayim: Ir Ha-Ḳodesh veha-Miḳdash—Ma'amarim*, edited by Jacob Gliss and Moshe Hayim Katzenelenbogen, 162–73. Jerusalem: Mosad Harav Kook, 1977.

Halamish, Moshe. "Birkat ha-Noten La-Ya'ef Koaḥ." *Asufot: Annual for Jewish Studies* 1 (1987): 361–77. [Hebrew]

———. *Kabbalah in Liturgy, Halakhah and Customs*. Ramat-Gan: Bar-Ilan University Press, 2000. [Hebrew]

Jacobson, Issachar (Bernhard Salomon). *Netiv Binah*. Vol. 1. 5 vols. Tel-Aviv: Sinai, 1964. [Hebrew]

Scholem, Gershom G. "The Paradisic Garb of Souls and the Origin of the Concept of 'Haluka de-Rabbanan.'" *Tarbiz* 24, no. 3 (1955): 290–306.

Tabory, Joseph. "The Conflict of Halakhah and Prayer." *Tradition: A Journal of Orthodox Jewish Thought* 25, no. 1 (1989): 17–31.

What Will the Neighbours Think?

The traditional Jewish practice in congregational worship requires that the central prayer, known as the "Eighteen Benedictions (*Shemoneh 'Esreh*), be recited two times in the service. First It is whispered or mumbled quietly by the individual worshippers, and afterwards it is chanted out loud by the prayer leader on behalf of the congregation.

Considering that the prayer in question is quite a lengthy one, its double recitation can challenge the patience of participants who have other tasks to attend to in their daily schedules. Nevertheless, the repetition was a mainstay of Jewish liturgical practice. Its origins date back to the era when rabbinic Judaism insisted on a strict differentiation between the written Torah—a category that was essentially restricted to the books in the Bible—and the oral Torah that comprised all the other accepted religious traditions. Because the prayers were classified as part of the oral tradition, they could not be written down, and therefore had to be memorized or improvised.

The rabbis realized that in the absence of written texts, many Jews were probably not knowledgeable enough to recite the complex prayers on the spot; and this was the main reason for instituting the dual recitation: during the initial silent recitation, the more learned worshipers would address their Creator individually; and afterwards the prayer leader would recite the text aloud so that unschooled members of the community could fulfil their obligations by responding "amen" to his blessings.

As with several qualities of devout prayer, the sages of the Talmud traced this one back to the biblical figure of Hannah, the pious mother of the prophet Samuel, about whom it said: "she spake in her heart; only her lips moved, but her voice was not heard." The rabbis pointed to several spiritual ideals that are best expressed by means of silent meditation—including the implied trust in an all-knowing God who does not need to be shouted at, and the opportunity it provides to confess individual sins without fear of their becoming embarrassing public knowledge.

The post-talmudic leaders of the Babylonian academies, the *Ge'onim*, were generally inflexible about continuing that ancient ritual, and they refused to abandon it even in the face of extenuating circumstances, such as when not enough time remained to recite the full service within the permitted time limits, or on Rosh Hashanah or Yom Kippur when the lengthy and elaborate service greatly exceeded the capabilities of most worshippers to articulate their own silent versions of the prayer.

Notwithstanding all the commendable reasons and benefits that might attach to the convention of repeating the prayer, it also gave rise to several problems. For one thing, it was based on a division of the congregation into two distinct classes, the literate and the uneducated. Consequently, each class might feel some redundancy or resentment regarding the the portion of the service allotted to the other.

In the twelfth century an inquiry was addressed to Maimonides concerning a custom that had been introduced by a former cantor in an Egyptian town: of reciting both renditions aloud, but omitting from the first one the passages that may only be recited in the context of formal communal worship. Those passages—primarily, the "*Kedushah*" (holiness) blessing—would be included in the subsequent repetition by the prayer leader. The community had adopted this format as their norm.

A Jewish scholar visiting from a Christian land later proposed a different alternative that was supported by some of the locals: According to his reading of the talmudic sources, the circumstances that gave rise to the silent reading—especially the concern about penitents not confessing their transgressions aloud—were not pertinent in most situations. Moreover, it was arguable that someone who has already fulfilled his obligation by reciting the prayer quietly should henceforth be disqualified from reciting it again as the congregational prayer leader. For this reason, the visitor recommended that they completely abolish the silent prayer, and keep only the full cantor's intonation. The community chose to remain loyal to their homegrown custom of two spoken recitations.

Maimonides himself categorically rejected the community's practice, insisting that vocal recitation of a silent prayer is self-contradictory and defeats the original purpose of the practice.

As for the proposal to abolish the silent prayer, Maimonides noted that this would contravene the Talmud's ruling and the normative custom. Nevertheless he supported such a procedure, but for entirely different reasons. In fact, he urged that it be adopted with the explicit awareness that it constituted an innovative religious reform.

Like similar reforms that had been introduced by the sages of previous eras, this one would be justified by an urgent need to overcome a serious problem. The knowledgeable members of the community, once they had fulfilled their own liturgical obligations by whispering the silent prayer, felt that they had no reason to listen attentively to the ensuing public recitation; and instead they felt free to chat, stroll, spit and cough. The masses, who looked to the scholars for guidance, emulated their behaviour to the point of feeling free to walk out of the sanctuary.

In order to counteract this irreverent chaos, Maimonides ordained that the service should consist of only a single, orderly reading of the Eighteen Benedictions aloud, during which the learned and the unlettered alike would be required to be standing respectfully and carry out their obligations by mouthing the words along with the leader or by responding "amen" to each blessing.

The maintaining of respectful decorum is of course an important religious value at all times. However, Maimonides had an additional—and probably more pressing—concern that he wished to address through his proposal. He argued that the existing situation amounted to a desecration of God's name. Muslim neighbours, who cultivated orderly discipline in their own prayers, derided the boorish behaviour in the synagogues that seems to make a mockery of prayer. In justifying his departure from established practice he invoked the scriptural battle cry, "It is time, Lord, to act for thee: for they have made void thy law!"

A student of Maimonides appealed to his teacher for support in his efforts to impose the liturgical reform in Alexandria. This tampering with the accepted custom succeeded only in part. It was limited to the town's smaller "Babylonian" synagogue and excluded certain holy days for which the worshipers refused to abandon their cherished liturgical poetry. Nevertheless, it had provoked widespread and vehement hostility that was taking a long time to calm down. At any rate, Maimonides' son Abraham reported that his father's enactment was taking hold in many middle eastern communities, a trend that would persist until the sixteenth century.

Maimonides' reform would be revisited by Rabbi David Ibn Abu Zimra [the Radbaz] who presided over the Jewish community of Egypt in the sixteenth century. In 1539 a dispute broke out between the new Sephardic majority who wished to restore the silent prayer, and the "native" Arabic-speaking ("*musta'rib*") Jewish community who insisted that residents of Maimonides' own city ought to remain loyal to his teaching.

In discussing Maimonides' arguments about maintaining a favourable impression among their Muslim neighbours, the Radbaz noted that the formerly respectful relations between Jews and Muslims had deteriorated significantly since Maimonides' day. "They dismiss our prayers as blasphemies, they claim that our Torah has been tampered with, and so forth. And since they hold such opinions about us anyway, we may as well just follow the normative law, since there would be no advantage to doing otherwise." It appears that this hostile attitude has only intensified since the Radbaz's days.

Now I do not normally encourage worrying about how others see us. Nonetheless, a bit more mutual respect between the two communities could well be an improvement.

Improbable as that objective appears at this point in history, it might yet be worth devoting a prayer for its achievement—at the least, a silent prayer.

Bibliography:

Blidstein, Gerald J. *Prayer in Maimonidean Halakha*. Jerusalem and Beersheba: Mosad Bialik and Ben-Gurion University of the Negev Press, 1994. [Hebrew]

Elbogen, Ismar. *Jewish Liturgy: A Comprehensive History*. Translated by Raymond P. Scheindlin. Philadelphia and New York: Jewish Publication Society and the Jewish Theological Seminary of America, 1993.

Friedlaender, Israel. "A New Responsum of Maimonides Concerning the Repetition of the 'Shmoneh Esreh.'" *The Jewish Quarterly Review* 5, no. 1 (1914): 1–15.

Friedman, Mordechai A. "Abraham Maimonides on His Leadership, Reforms, and Spiritual Imperfection." *Jewish Quarterly Review* 104, no. 3 (2014): 495–512.

———. "Abraham Maimuni's Prayer Reforms: Continuation or Revision of His Father's Teachings?" In *Traditions of Maimonideanism*, edited by Carlos Fraenkel, 139–54. Leiden: Brill, 2009.

———. "Repetition of the Evening ʿAmīda on Festivals and Special Sabbaths in the Custom of Eretz Israel." *Tarbiz* 85, no. 3 (2018): 477–93.

Halamish, Moshe. "Siḥit Ḥullin be-Veit-Keneset: Metsi'ut u-Ma'avaḳ." *MILET: Studies in Jewish History and Culture* 2 (1974): 225–51.

Morell, Samuel. *Studies in the Judicial Methodology of Rabbi David Ibn Abi Zimra*. Studies in Judaism. Dallas: University Press of America, 2004.

Reif, Stefan C. "Maimonides on the Prayers." In *Traditions of Maimonideanism*, edited by Carlos Fraenkel, 73–100. Leiden: Brill, 2009.

———. *Problems with Prayers: Studies in the Textual History of Early Rabbinic Liturgy*. Studia Judaica 37. Berlin and New York: W. de Gruyter, 2006.

Wieder, Naphtali. *Islamic Influences on the Jewish Worship*. Oxford: Sifriyyat Mizraḥ u-Maʿarav, 1947. [Hebrew]

Testing the Waters

I suppose that most of us have almost identical visual images of Noah's ark. We envisage it as a large houseboat with rounded contours and an upper deck occupied mainly by African animals, especially the obligatory giraffe.

Although that depiction might be ubiquitous in cartoons and children's toys, it hardly fits the description found in the Bible itself. In fact, the craft that Noah built was not designated as a ship or boat at all, but as a container or box (as indicated correctly by the English "ark"). It was a rectangular structure three hundred by fifty by thirty cubits (137 × 22.9 × 13.7 meters), tapering to a point towards its top (useful for draining the torrential rain). A statement in the midrash noted that these proportions were ideal for ensuring the stability of a vessel at rest in harbour; and this was consistent with the construction practices for Roman merchant galleys. The ark was, at any rate, comparable to the cubic craft constructed by Utnapishtim to survive the flood, as related in the Babylonian "Epic of Gilgamesh."

Now, the Torah provides what seems at first glance to be a clear and precise timetable of the various stages of the rainfall, the rising and receding of the waters, and the ark's eventual settling onto Mount Ararat. For some of the stages it counts the numbers of days, whereas in other instances it identifies them by the dates in the months. Unfortunately, months in biblical parlance did not have names, but were referred to by numbers, and it is not always clear how the counting is being done. Does the "seventh month" refer to a fixed calendar—and if so, would that be the normal biblical calendar beginning in the spring with Nissan, or the alternate system that begins with Tishri in the fall? Or is it just counting the months from the last-mentioned point in the narrative?

The rabbis of the midrash provided a chronology according to which the divine judgment of that wicked generation extended for exactly twelve months. Perhaps this was regarded as a prototype for the sentences that are meted out to all of us sinners after death.

The Torah says that the water level at the flood's peak was at least fifteen cubits. According to the rabbis' calculations, the ark came to rest after the waters had receded only four cubits. From this premise they deduced that part of the craft—the bottom eleven cubits—must have been submerged under the water as it floated. This would prevent it from keeling over, and makes good nautical sense. It might reflect the sages' familiarity with the structures of the boats in the Sea of Galilee or the Mediterranean; though it is not clear why they felt obliged to raise this technical matter in a religious commentary.

In the eleventh century in France, Rashi included a paraphrase of that complicated midrashic calculation in his commentary to the Torah, supplemented by his own justification for the rabbis' identifications of the various months in the biblical chronology. This all seems perfectly reasonable. Rashi often elucidated scriptural passages in accordance with the ancient rabbinic interpretations.

And yet when we advance to thirteenth century Catalonia, we find that Rabbi Moses ben Nahman (Nahmanides, Ramban) was not at all pleased with Rashi's judgment in this matter. He frowned upon Rashi's eclectic propensity to fluctuate between literal explanations and midrashic expositions. Invoking the talmudic proposition that "there are seventy facets to the Torah," Nahmanides allowed himself to challenge Rashi (and the midrash), and argue for a different reading of the biblical text. With that in mind, he attacked Rashi for his inconsistency in attaching different meanings to the Torah's various enumerations of months in the passage.

Nahmanides also rejected the premise that water recedes at a steady, unchanging rate. This seemed unlikely, especially when applied to uneven mountainous terrain. Furthermore, Noah's ark was a flat-bottom craft with its top section narrowing to a single cubit in width. If more than one third of its lower portion were submerged beneath the surface of the water, it would not be seaworthy.

A very similar exegetical disagreement emerged a few generations later, but this time in the domain of Christian exegesis. The Franciscan scholar Nicholas de Lyra was the author of the "Postilla litteralis super totam Bibliam," which was completed in 1332 and went on to become the most widely read Christian commentary to the Bible. In his notes to the Noah narrative in Genesis, de Lyra boasted that, based on the dates and numbers provided in the scriptural account, it was possible to compute how much of the ark was submerged under the water. His calculation came to nine or thirteen cubits.

From Postillae perpetuae in universam S. Scripturam. 15th Century, Bibliothèque Nationale de France

Almost a century later, in 1429, the learned Castilian expositor Pablo de Santa Maria of Burgos completed a work devoted to criticism of de Lyra's interpretations: "Aditiones ad postillam Magistri Nicolai Lyra." Pablo was particularly concerned to set distinct methodological boundaries between literal and allegorical readings.

Pablo objected vehemently to de Lyra's discussion about the receding of the waters and the dimensions of the ark's submersion. For one thing, the trivial exercise in deduction served no useful purpose in steering the reader toward correct beliefs or practical moral behaviour—in effect, Pablo was claiming that Nicholas had gotten in over his head. Without going into precise argumentation, he claimed that the biblical text was open to other and better interpretations.

It is no coincidence that the controversy among these Christian exegetes bore such an uncanny similarity to the to the one between Rashi and Nahmanides. Nicholas de Lyra was a devoted admirer of Rashi, and courteous references to "Rabbi Salomon" appear on just about every page of his lengthy commentary. In Nicholas' eyes, Rashi was the epitome of reasonable Jewish literal exegesis. It was probably through Nicholas' subsequent influence on Christian biblical studies that the King James English translation came to incorporate a great deal of traditional Jewish interpretation.

As for Pablo de Santa Maria—this prominent Catholic theologian and exegete had begun his career as Rabbi Solomon Ha-Levi. He converted to Christianity in 1391, apparently out of sincere religious conviction; though many other Spanish Jews were accepting baptism on account of the large-scale massacres that were being perpetrated at that time. Pablo rose to important positions in the universities, the church and in the government of Castile, and he took an aggressive part in attempts to convert or persecute his former coreligionists.

It has been suggested that with respect to his exegetical approach, Pablo's opposition was not so much to Nicholas de Lyra himself, but to his excessive reliance on Rashi. Or, to put it another way: even after abandoning his ancestral faith, Pablo continued to uphold the persistent scholarly rivalry between the French and Sephardic approaches to scriptural interpretation. The Sephardic authors had developed their own rigorous system of grammatical and literary methods for uncovering the original meanings of the sacred texts; and they often felt that it was unfair that Rashi should be treated by northern European Jews and Christians as the doyen of literal exegesis. Nicholas' tacit reliance on Rashi's analysis of the ark's dimensions and nautical state (he seemed unaware that Rashi was in fact paraphrasing an earlier midrashic source) exemplified his own shortcomings, as well as Rashi's failure to maintain the distinctions between literal and midrashic hermeneutical methodologies.

In choosing which of the competing interpretations is the better one, it is of course necessary to examine the specific merits and weaknesses of each, noting how well it accounts for the linguistic usages and the narrative logic of the scriptural text.

And yet, as we saw in this example, there are often ulterior motives that influence exegetes in their work. These motives are not usually stated explicitly, and the authors might not even be consciously aware of them.

But like the hulls of sailing craft, they are often lying beneath the surface.

Bibliography:

Baer, Yitzhak. *A History of the Jews in Christian Spain*. Philadelphia: Jewish Publication Society, 1992.

Elman, Yaakov. "'It Is No Empty Thing': Nahmanides and the Search for Omnisignificance." *The Torah U-Madda Journal* 4 (1993): 1–83.

Geiger, Ari. "A Student and an Opponent. Nicholas of Lyra and His Jewish Sources." In *Nicolas De Lyre Franciscain Du XIV Siè Exégète et Théologien*, edited by Gilbert Dahan and Louis Burle, 167–203. Collection Des Études Augustiniennes: Série Moyen Âge et Temps Modernes 48. Paris: Institut d'Études Augustiniennes, 2011.

Hailperin, Herman. *Rashi and the Christian Scholars*. Pittsburgh: University of Pittsburgh Press, 1963.

Klepper, Deeana Copeland. *The Insight of Unbelievers: Nicholas of Lyra and Christian Reading of Jewish Text in the Later Middle Ages*. Jewish Culture and Contexts. Philadelphia: University of Pennsylvania Press, 2007.

Merrill, Eugene H. "Rashi, Nicholas De Lyra, and Christian Exegesis." *The Westminster Theological Journal* 38, no. 1 (1975): 66–79.

Milikowsky, Chaim Joseph, ed. *Seder Olam: Critical Edition, Commentary, and Introduction*. Jerusalem: Yad Ben Zvi Press: Rabbi Moses and Amaliah Rosen Foundation, 2013. [Hebrew]

Netanyahu, Benzion. *The Origins of the Inquisition in Fifteenth Century Spain*. 1st edition. New York: Random House, 1995.

Sarna, Nahum M. *Understanding Genesis*. 1st ed. Heritage of Biblical Israel 1. New York: Jewish Theological Seminary of America, 1966.

Twersky, Isadore, ed. "Open Rebuke and Concealed Love: Nahmanides and the Andalusian Tradition." In *Rabbi Moses Naḥmanides (Ramban): Explorations in His Religious and Literary Virtuosity*, 11–34. Texts and Studies of the Harvard University Center for Jewish Studies 1. Cambridge, MA: Harvard University Press, 1983.

Smalley, Beryl. *The Study of the Bible in the Middle Ages*. Oxford: Clarendon Press, 1941.

Sperber, Daniel. *Nautica Talmudica*. Bar-Ilan Studies in Near Eastern Languages and Culture. Ramat-Gan, Israel: Bar-Ilan University Press, 1986.

Yisraeli, Yosi. "A Christianized Sephardic Critique of Rashi's Peshaṭ in Pablo de Santa Maria's Additiones Ad Postillam Nicolai de Lyra." In *Medieval Exegesis and Religious Difference: Commentary, Conflict, and Community in the Premodern Mediterranean*, edited by Ryan Szpiech, First edition., 128–41. Bordering Religions: Concepts, Conflicts, and Conversations. New York: Fordham University Press, 2015.

The Unkindness of Strangers

According to the story told in the book of Genesis, the cities of Sodom and Gomorrah were condemned to destruction because the outcry against them was "so great and their sin so grievous." Not even a bare quorum of ten righteous persons could be found to justify averting the catastrophe.

The Torah does not tell us what exactly were those grievous sins that warranted the cities' devastation by brimstone and fire. In English parlance, as in most Christian-based traditions, the event generated the word "sodomy" to designate sexual offences, inferred from the passage where the men of the city surrounded Lot's house and threatened his angelic visitors: "Where are the men which came in to thee this night? Bring them out unto us, that we may know them!"

As appalling as that episode may be, it was not what defined Sodom's immorality in most ancient Hebrew traditions. The prophets of Israel frequently invoked Sodom as a benchmark for their own people's moral failings and as an object lesson for the ruin that Israel was inviting upon itself. Ezekiel gave the most explicit listing of those sins: "Behold, this was the iniquity of thy sister Sodom: pride, fulness of bread, and abundance of idleness was in her and in her daughters, neither did she strengthen the hand of the poor and needy." That city, which had enjoyed the luxuries and indolence that come from material affluence, became insensitive to the plight of the disadvantaged. This was the evil that had justified Sodom's annihilation—and according to the prophet, the complacent Judeans of his generation deserved no better. With an insight that sounds disturbingly contemporary, a rabbinic tradition observed how Sodom's wealthy gentry resented having to share their wealth with shabby immigrant newcomers.

G. Doré, Lot Flees as Sodom and Gomorrah Burn

A passage in the Talmud relates several anecdotes about the injustices that prevailed in Sodom. Most of those stories sound like comical folk tales about a topsy-turvy legal system in which corrupt magistrates impose penalties on innocent victims, though in some cases a resourceful trickster (notably Abraham's servant Eliezer) was able to turn the tables on the reprobates. In keeping with the biblical sources, several of the Talmud's tales are about the mistreatment of guests, visitors, widows and orphans. The collection includes an adaptation of the well-known Greek legend about Procrustes, the fiendish bandit who forced guests to fit into his one-size-fits-none iron bed even if it required painful stretching or amputating their limbs.

The Sodomite mentality is depicted somewhat differently in the discourse of rabbinic law and ethics.

Mishnah Avot 5:10 according to MS Kaufmann, Budapest

Various situations were discussed in which one party asks another for a favour that would benefit him without imposing any disadvantage on the other. For example, if somebody has taken up residence in a house whose owner had no intention of living in it himself or renting it out, can the owner claim payment from the squatter? Or: how should we deal with a case where Reuben intends to sell a field that borders on Simeon's property, and Simeon requests that his offer be given priority because it would be especially convenient for him to be cultivating a single continuous property. For Reuben to refuse this kind of request—apparently out of spite or meanness—is stigmatized by the Talmud as "the standard of Sodom"; and the sages discuss whether a Jewish court can compel Reuben to accede to Simeon's request. Everyone seems to agree that such coercion is legitimate in principle. The only quibbles that occupy the scholars are about how to measure the benefits or disadvantages to the respective litigants in particular cases.

The general tendency among subsequent authorities has been to recognize even small, temporary or hypothetical annoyances as overriding the consideration of "the standard of Sodom."

Although the civil justice system in modern Israel draws most of its legal precedents from the British Common Law tradition, the 1980 "Foundations of Law Act" authorized the courts to give consideration to "the principles of freedom, justice, equity, and peace of Israel's heritage." It is interesting to note that several judicial decisions have invoked the talmudic rule about using compulsion against the "standard of Sodom" in order to promote a kind of natural justice, even when this seemed opposed to the prevailing Common Law approach.

A more theoretical or psychological perspective on the phenomenon is found in the Mishnah tractate *Avot* ("Ethics of the Fathers"). The Mishnah enumerates different human attitudes towards personal property, ranging from the extreme magnanimity of one who declares "what is mine is yours and what is yours is yours" to the rapacious "what is mine is mine and what is yours is mine." After noting that the stance of "what is mine is mine and what is yours is yours" is that of a normal person, the Mishnah records a dissenting opinion that in fact "this is the standard of Sodom"!

Not surprisingly, this disagreement generated quite a bit of discussion among Jewish thinkers and commentators. It might come as a surprise to many of us that most Jewish thinkers favoured the second view in the Mishnah, and had difficulty justifying the first opinion.

Typical of such writers was the thirteenth-century halakhist and moralist Rabbi Jonah of Gerona. While he can readily accept that a person's reluctance to be on the receiving end of generosity is consistent with the counsel in the Book of Proverbs that "he that hateth gifts shall live," he finds it inconceivable that the sages would rank a Jew who refuses to give charity as anything less than wicked, especially in light of Ezekiel's explicit condemnation of such persons.

Rabbi Jonah therefore proposed that the Mishnah was not speaking about persons who refrain entirely from any charitable giving (these misers are unquestionably to be stigmatized for their Sodom-like baseness), but rather about those who have to force themselves to be generous against their natural inclinations. The underlying question is whether we judge such people negatively, on the basis of their uncaring feelings (which will lead to widespread social evils if they are not duly criticized)—or respectfully, in deference to their dutiful, albeit reluctant, actions.

Rabbi Simeon Duran of Algiers argued that the Mishnah was not speaking about charitable giving at all, but about relations among social equals. A misanthropic insistence on complete self-sufficiency might be an acceptable ideal (as exemplified by some righteous figures in the Bible) provided that one does perform some acts of benevolence. However, the author of the Mishnah's second opinion was worried that such behaviour might develop into the severely anti-social attitudes associated with the citizens of Sodom.

The "to each his own" attitude is indeed the norm of classical laissez-faire political thought, according to which a person's right to honestly earned possessions is sacred and the Powers-That-Be should have little or no business redistributing such assets. If I choose to be generous with my wealth, that is my own decision, but it cannot be subject to judicial coercion. In our culturally diverse world, most of us are understandably wary of governments forcing their morals or beliefs down our throats.

On the other hand, our world appears to have swerved to the opposite extreme. We have come to believe that any act that is not actually punishable by law is socially acceptable; and there is no longer any level of personal disgrace that would necessitate a politician's resignation or dismissal.

Such ethical dilemmas, like the human situation itself, are inherently complex and subject to varying circumstances. They certainly do not lend themselves to homogeneous solutions—and they should not be forced into inflexible Procrustean beds,

Bibliography:

Elon, Menachem. *Jewish Law: History, Sources, Principles*. 3 vols. Philadelphia: Jewish Publication Society, 1994.

Englard, Izhak. "The Problem of Jewish Law in a Jewish State." *Israel Law Review* 3, no. 2 (1968): 254–78.

Epstein-Halevi, Elimelech. *Sha'arei Ha-'Aggadah*. Tel-Aviv: Dvir, 1982. [Hebrew]

Ginzberg, Louis. *Legends of the Jews*. Translated by Henrietta Szold. 2nd ed. Philadelphia: Jewish Publication Society of America, 2003.

Lichtenstein, Aharon. "'Kofin Al Middat Sedom': Compulsory Altruism?" Edited by Reuven Ziegler. Translated by David Strauss. *Alei Etzion: A Torah Periodical of Yeshivat Har Etzion* 16, [Special Issue in Honor of Harav Aharon Lichtenstein] (2009): 31–70.

Segal, Eliezer. "A Funny Thing Happened on My Way to Sodom." *Journal for the Study of Judaism in the Persian, Hellenistic, and Roman Period* 46, no. 1 (2015): 103–29.

Shilo, Shmuel. "Kofin Al Midat S'dom: Jewish Law's Concept of Abuse of Rights." *Israel Law Review* 15, no. 1 (1980): 49–78.

Ta-Shma, Israel M. "Rabbi Jonah Gerondi: Spirituality and Leadership." In *Creativity and Tradition: Studies in Medieval Rabbinic Scholarship, Literature and Thought*, 213–27.

Cambridge MA: Distributed by Harvard University Press for Harvard University Center for Jewish Studies, 2007.

Zevin, Shelomoh Josef. "Zeh Neheneh veZeh Lo Ḥaser." Edited by Shelomoh Josef Zevin. *Talmudic Encyclopedia*. Jerusalem: Talmudic Encyclopedia Institute, 1978. [Hebrew]

Speed Demon

Jewish law establishes limitations about where and how far one may travel and carry on the Sabbaths or holy days. These laws are rooted in the passage in the book of Exodus that tells of the miraculous mannah, the "bread from heaven" that nourished the Israelites during their sojourn in the desert. Mannah would not materialize on the Sabbath, and the people were admonished not to leave their dwellings to look for it: "Abide ye every man in his place, let no man go out of his place on the seventh day." What may have originated as a warning to trust the divine word was understood by the Jewish legal tradition as a categorical prohibition against traveling beyond a specified distance from one's place of residence or carrying objects between private and public domains.

Rabbi Ḥanina in the Talmud raised the intriguing question of whether the legal distinctions between the different domains apply only on the surface level; or do they extend above-ground—beyond the elevation of ten hand-breaths that normally defines the upper limit of a private domain? What was at that time a trifling instance of unrealistic rabbinic casuistry would later take on practical relevance for dealing with air rights in our age of aviation and drones.

In its effort to resolve Rabbi Ḥanina's query, the Talmud cited an incident that occurred in the academies of fourth-century Babylonia. One Saturday morning, a collection of seven statements was expounded before Rav Ḥisda in the town of Sura, and towards the end of that day the exact same statements were cited before Rava in Pumbedita (today's Fallujah), some 175 km away! The best explanation that the rabbis could produce for that instantaneous transfer of the teachings over such a large distance was by postulating supernatural channels of communication.

Jewish lore knows of one prominent figure who travels between the earthly and heavenly domains, namely the prophet Elijah. Scripture does not tell of Elijah's death, but rather of his ascent to heaven in a whirlwind with a chariot of fire. Rabbinic literature relates many conversations between the prophet and Jewish sages, and it was therefore not entirely unreasonable for them to suppose that Elijah had couriered the teachings from Sura to Pumbedita. Since he was of course observant of Jewish law, he could not have walked beyond the permitted limits. Therefore, they initially assumed that he flew the distance (perhaps in a chariot or whirlwind). However, this explanation only works if we accept the premise that there is not any Sabbath no-fly zone in effect above ground level. This reasoning would appear to answer Rabbi Ḥanina's question.

However, the Talmud rejects that argument. The Elijah hypothesis is not the only plausible way of accounting for the same-day delivery of Rav Ḥisda's seven statements. The ancient rabbis knew of at least one other figure who could have traversed the distance: "Perhaps it was Joseph the demon who reported them!" Rashi explained that the demon was not subject to the objections leveled against Elijah because he was not Sabbath-observant.

The mention of a demon in an ancient Jewish text is hardly remarkable, since until quite recently virtually every known human culture shared the belief in invisible beings who have to be controlled or conciliated (In our more scientifically advanced civilization we assign similar roles to space aliens, viruses and Google). The Iranian heritage that held sway in Babylonia at that time was particularly rich in its mythology of subversive and malevolent "daevas," and this is vividly reflected in the Talmud.

It is nonetheless interesting that the supernatural creature mentioned in this story bears a Hebrew name, and that the venues of his activities were rabbinic academies. It is not clear whether he was motivated by a helpful desire to advance the spread of Torah learning, or if he was colluding in a kind of plagiaristic hacking into proprietary Suran knowledge.

This is not the only place in the Talmud that mentions Joseph the demon. For the most part, he appears as a sympathetic figure, one who makes use of his demonic connections to assist the Jewish sages. Thus, Rav Pappa and Rav quote him as a source of practical first-hand advice about how to protect oneself from the machinations of evil spirits who are ready to attack the unfortunate persons who committed the deadly blunder of imbibing or performing other actions in even-numbered units.

Jewish rationalists were understandably reluctant to accept this kind of story at face value. The thirteenth-century Provençal scholar Rabbi Menaḥem Meiri asserted that the Talmud's reference to Elijah was purely figurative; it alluded to a contemporary teacher—albeit one who was capable of leaping between distant towns like the biblical prophet. Similarly, for Meiri Joseph was not literally a demon. Like all such instances in rabbinic literature, that epithet was being employed here as a rhetorical euphemism to indicate a Jew who violated the Sabbath, and perhaps to contrast him with the proverbial "Joseph who honours the Sabbath," the devout hero of a well-known talmudic tale.

Rabbi Judah the Pious of Regensburg, the foremost figure in the medieval mystical "Ḥasidei Ashkenaz" movement, insisted that not only do demons believe in the Torah, but they even scrupulous in their observance of all the rabbinic laws. When challenged as to how Joseph was able to transmit his information from Sura to Pumbedita without transgressing the Sabbath laws, Rabbi Judah explained that Joseph in fact never left Pumbedita, where he received the data from a fellow demon stationed in Sura who communicated it to him by means of a "long hollow tablet."

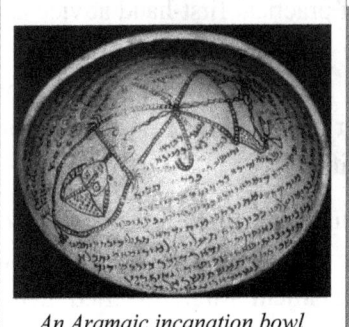

An Aramaic incanation bowl

I am not sure how exactly we are supposed to visualize that ancient communication device. Apparently Rabbi Judah had in mind an ultra-long tube capable of conveying and sustaining a voice over vast distances (He was probably not aware of the actual distance involved). In any case, Rabbi Judah's disciple Rabbi Isaac Or Zarua' challenged his teacher's explanation, pointing out that as long as there was no Sabbath desecration involved, then there was no reason for the Talmud to abandon its initial hypothesis that it was Elijah who conveyed the information to Pumbedita.

Our knowledge of talmudic Judaism in Babylonia derives almost exclusively from the information contained in the Talmud itself, with very few external archeological artifacts. An interesting exception to this rule is the phenomenon of "incantation bowls." These are clay bowls whose interior surfaces are inscribed with magical texts in Aramaic, usually written in a continuous spiral beginning from the outer rim. These were intended to restrain or expel hostile demonic beings. The bowls would be placed upside-down so that they would symbolically entrap their supernatural targets. Thousands of these bowls have been unearthed, mostly around Nippur. Most of them are of Jewish provenance, and their wording is often modeled after Jewish legal formulas, especially those that are employed in documents of divorce or excommunications. There are certain rabbis whose names are standardly invoked in the incantations, but these are usually legendary figures who lived long before the time when the bowls were produced.

However, one of those bowls—after listing an impressive roster of figures who endorse the ban, continues: "...And may you be under the ban of **Rav** Joseph the demon. And may you be under the ban of all demons and dark ones that are in Babylonia."

For the scribe who composed this incantation, Joseph the demon was not merely an observant Jew (as would later be claimed by Rabbi Judah the Pious), but he even qualified for a rabbinic ordination and the title "Rav"—Rabbi. Evidently the two callings were not regarded as mutually contradictory.

And his sermons might not have been original, but they were probably delivered very quickly.

Bibliography:

Halbertal, Moshe. *Between Torah and Wisdom: Rabbi Menachem Ha-Meiri and the Maimonidean Halakhists in Provence.* Jerusalem: Magnes Press, 2000. [Hebrew]

Harari, Yuval. *Early Jewish Magic: Research, Method, Sources.* Jerusalem: Mosad Bialik, Ben Zvi Institute for the Study of Jewish Communities in the East, Yad Ben-Zvi, the Hebrew University of Jerusalem, 2010. [Hebrew]

———. *Jewish Magic before the Rise of Kabbalah.* 1st edition. Raphael Patai Series in Jewish Folklore and Anthropology. Detroit, MI: Wayne State University Press, 2017.

Harviainen, Tipani. *An Aramaic Incantation Bowl from Borsippa: Another Specimen of Eastern Aramaic "Koiné."* Studia Orientalia Edited by the Finnish Oriental Society. Helsinki: Federation of Finnish Learned Societies, 1981.

Ilan, Tal. "Rav Joseph the Demon in the Rabbinic Academy in Babylonia: Another Connection between the Babylonian Talmud and the Magic Bowls." In *Let the Wise Listen and Add to Their Learning (Prov. 1:5): Festschrift for Günter Stemberger on the Occasion of His 75th Birthday*, edited by Günter Stemberger, Constanza Cordoni, and Gerhard Langer, 381–94. Studia Judaica 90. Berlin ; Boston: De Gruyter, 2016.

Levene, Dan. *Jewish Aramaic Curse Texts from Late-Antique Mesopotamia: "May These Curses Go Out and Flee."* Magical and Religious Literature of Late Antiquity 2. Leiden: Brill, 2014.

Lindbeck, Kristen H. *Elijah and the Rabbis: Story and Theology.* New York: Columbia University Press, 2010.

Montgomery, James Alan, ed. *Aramaic Incantation Texts from Nippur.* Philadelphia: University Museum, 1913.

Secunda, Shai. *The Iranian Talmud: Reading the Bavli in Its Sasanian Context*. 1st ed. Philadelphia: University of Pennsylvania Press, 2014.

Shaked, Shaul. "Form and Purpose in Aramaic Spells: Some Jewish Themes [the Poetics of Magic Texts]." In *Officina Magica: Essays on the Practice of Magic in Antiquity*, 1–30. Leiden and Boston: Brill, 2005.

Shaked, Shaul, James Nathan Ford, and Siam Bhayro. *Aramaic Bowl Spells: Jewish Babylonian Aramaic Bowls*. Magical and Religious Literature of Late Antiquity 20. Leiden and Boston: Brill, 2013.

Steinsaltz, Adin. *The Essential Talmud*. Translated by Chaya Galai. New York: Basic Books, 1976.

It's My Party—and You'll Cry If I Want to

One of the happiest expressions in the vocabulary of Hebrew-speakers, especially the young and young-at-heart, is *"yom huledet"*—birthday. The term has a long history, making its debut in the book of Genesis in the context of the Joseph story. During his incarceration in the Egyptian dungeon, the young Hebrew interpreted the dreams of his fellow prisoners, the chief butler and chief baker; and then, "it came to pass the third day, which was Pharaoh's birthday, that he made a feast unto all his servants: and he lifted up the head of the chief butler and of the chief baker among his servants."

The occasion has all the ingredients of a familiar birthday celebration, including a party and the fulfilment of wishes—though I suppose that an absolute monarch like Pharaoh could have his wishes fulfilled on every day of the year. All that's missing is a cake adorned with candles and icing and a game of Pin-the-Tail-on-Seth-Typhon-the Donkey-Headed-God.

Though for modern Israelis the words "*yom huledet*" roll-easily off the tongue, the biblical usage is far from simple. Grammarians point to its incongruous status as a passive infinitive, which should not take an object; and yet Pharaoh's name is introduced here by the Hebrew particle "*et*" that usually indicates a direct object. This could imply that the birth that was being celebrated was not that of the current Pharaoh, but perhaps that of a newborn heir to the throne. Indeed, the grammarian and lexicographer Rabbi David Kimhi seemed undecided as to whether Pharaoh was marking the birth of a son or an annual commemoration of his own birth. Rashi analyzed the wording at considerable length in order to defend the interpretation that this was Pharaoh's own birthday party. Towards the end of his comment he explained the syntactic logic, and he provided examples of similar usages in biblical Hebrew.

The Greek Septuagint translation has "the day of Pharaoh's *geneseos.*" The same Greek word is used by the Midrash *Genesis Rabbah* and in some of the Aramaic Targums. Rashi also equates *yom huledet* with the term "*genesia*" that appears in rabbinic texts. The Mishnah contains a list of days on which Jews should avoid doing business with pagans, so as not to give them occasion for rejoicing or expressing gratitude to their idols. One of the items on the list is "the king's *genesia* day."

The Greek word "*genesia*" is well known from classical

literature. It was mentioned by Herodotus in connection with the festivities that were observed by dutiful Greek sons in honor of their deceased fathers—evidently on their birthdays. However, there is no lack of instances where that word refers to birthdays of the living. The first-century Jewish philosopher Philo of Alexandria employed a similar word (*genesthia*) to describe the seventh day of the creation as a universal celebration of the "birthday of the world." Now, the creator of the universe, we must not forget, is normally portrayed as its supreme monarch.

The question thus arises, whether birthday celebrations were perceived in the classical sources as an exclusive prerogative of emperors and pharaohs, or whether they could be enjoyed by commoners as well.

In this connection it is significant that the sages in the Mishnah associated the forbidden imperial birthdays with the burning of corpses. In Roman practice this ritual was part of the process of "Apotheosis" by which an emperor assumed divine status upon his death. His body and a wax effigy were burned on a tall funeral pyre, from the top of which an eagle was dispatched to carry the monarch's soul to its celestial abode. In subsequent years his birthday would be commemorated annually in solemn ceremonies. Many of the pagan practices and objects forbidden by rabbinic law were those associated with the cult of emperor worship, for which the talmudic sages had an intense distaste.

Non-royal birthdays are mentioned less frequently in classical documents. Nevertheless, there exists a considerable literature of Latin birthday greetings addressed to the authors' social superiors (and at times just to friends), invoking blessings and gratitude upon them and their guardian spirits ("*genius*"; in Hebrew: "*mazal*"). We learn from these texts about the cultic rituals—including sacrifices, libations, incense, wreaths and ritual cakes—that accompanied the patron's "*dies natalis*." Indeed, such religiously observed birthdays appear to have been an important component of the patronage system that was central to the Roman social structure.

A tyrant's behaviour at his party could be—well, tyrannical. True, Pharaoh's birthday feast proved to be a propitious step in Joseph's rise to success, but I doubt that the chief baker would have seen it quite that way as he was being led to his execution.

Several of those ancient royal celebrations involved disastrous consequences for Jews. Antiochos IV's birthday was the occasion for the decree in which he compelled his subjects, on pain of death, to participate in the cult of Bacchus in the Temple. The Roman general (later emperor) Titus Flavius, the destroyer of Jerusalem, made the birthdays of his brother and father occasions for the deadly party games for which his nation was infamous: condemning thousands of Jews to horrible fates in the arenas by ferocious beasts, gladiatorial combat and other forms of suffering and death.

And then there was the unfortunate case of the itinerant preacher John the Baptist who provoked the rage of Herod Antipas, tetrarch of the Galilee, by challenging the legitimacy of his marriage to his sister-in-law Herodias. According to the Christian account, it was at the ruler's birthday celebration (*genesia*) that Herodias's daughter Salomé performed the dance that induced him to grant her the fulfilment of a wish "up to half my kingdom"—which turned out (at her mother's suggestion) to be the delivery of John's head on a platter (in a manner that might have been meant to evoke Pharaoh's "lifting up" the head of the chief baker).

It appears from the discussions of several later Jewish interpreters that birthday celebrations were largely a privilege reserved for royalty. This seems to be the view of the fifteenth-century Yemenite exegete Rabbi Zechariah the Physician who mentioned the widespread custom of holding a feast on the king's birthday.

And who says that birthdays have to be limited to once a year? Another Yemenite scholar, Nethanel ben Isaiah, the fourteenth-century compiler of the book *Ma'or Afelah*, wrote that "kings used to hold feasts on the same day of the week on which they were born. For example, whoever was born on Saturday would make a feast every Saturday." Living in an Islamic environment, Nethanel had little knowledge of Christianity (which he dismissed as idolatrous), and he inferred that their observance of Sunday as a weekly holy day was because it was the commemoration of Jesus's birthday. (In reality, the Sunday "Lord's Day" derived its sanctity from being the day of his resurrection.)

There were nonetheless some commentators who were aware that birthdays could also be celebrated by commoners.

Rabbi Menahem ben Solomon, the twelfth-century Italian author of the "*Sekhel Ṭov*" commentary to the Torah, remarked with reference to Pharaoh's birthday that "Most people have a fondness for the day when they complete a year of their life, the anniversary of their birth. They are happy about it and hold a feast."

In his ethical will, Rabbi Israel Lipschutz (1782-1860) commanded all of his seven children to send each other congratulatory greetings on every birthday —and he made sure to list all their dates. "And it goes without saying that all greetings must be acknowledged. No exceptions except for unavoidable circumstances."

Rabbi Israel Lipschutz

He made no mention of piñatas or bouncy castles.

Bibliography:

Argetsinger, Kathryn. "Birthday Rituals: Friends and Patrons in Roman Poetry and Cult." *Classical Antiquity* 11, no. 2 (1992): 175–93.

Blaufuss, Johannes. *Römische Feste und Feiertage nach den Traktaten über fremden Dienst (Aboda zara) in Mischna, Tosefta, Jerusalemer und babylonischen Talmud*. Beilage zum

Jahresberichte des Königl. Neuen Gymnasiums in Nürnberg. Nürnberg: J. Stich, 1909.

Deblytzki, Serayah. "Ba'al Tif'eret Yisra'el u- Şva'ato." *Hama'yan* 11, no. 4 (1971): 28–44. [Hebrew]

Elmslie, Alexander Leslie, ed. *The Mishna on Idolatry*. Cambridge UK: Cambridge University Press, 1911.

Krauss, Samuel. *Paras Ve-Romi Ba-Talmud Uva-Midrashim*. Jerusalem: Mossad Harav Kook, 1948. [Hebrew]

Lachs, Samuel Tobias. "A Note on Genesia in Abodah Zara I,3." *The Jewish Quarterly Review* 58, no. 1 (1967): 69–71.

Rosenthal, David. "Mishna Aboda Zara — A Critical Edition with an Introduction." The Hebrew University, 1981.

Schürer, Emil. "17. The Sons of Herod." In *A History of the Jewish People in the Time of Jesus*, edited by Géza Vermès, Fergus Millar, and Martin Goodman, 2:10–149. London, New Delhi, New York, Sydney: Bloomsbury T. & T. Clark, 2014.

Ta-Shma, Israel M. "On Birthdays in Judaism." *Zion* 67, no. 1 (2002): 19–24. [Hebrew]

Ulmer, Rivka, and Brigitte Kern-Ulmer. "Visions of Egypt in Midrash: 'Pharaoh's Birthday' and the 'Nile Festival'." In *Biblical Interpretation in Judaism and Christianity*, edited by Isaac Kalimi and Peter J. Haas, 52–78. Library of Hebrew Bible/Old Testament Studies 439. New York: T & T Clark, 2006.

Urbach, Efraim Elimelech. "The Rabbinical Laws of Idolatry in the Second and Third Centuries in the Light of Archaeological and Historical Facts." *Israel Exploration Journal* 9, no. 3 (1959): 149–65.

Dead Men Don't Sneeze

As I write this article, the Canadian climate is striving to live up to its reputation for icy frigidity. For many us, this situation expresses itself in sneezes. As I understand it, a sneeze is physical defense mechanism that rids the nostrils of unwanted irritants and germs by forcibly expelling them in a spasmodic release of air and mucus.

Aside from the physiological aspects of sternutation (that is the fancy medical term), the reflex also has a remarkable social characteristic. It triggers a verbal response from those who are present during the explosive event. The most familiar responses according to western etiquette are "(God) Bless you" and "Gesundheit."

The popularity of the first expression has diminished with the secularization of our society—though a notorious 2014

Fox News report about a student's suspension for uttering it in a Tennessee public high school turned out to be inaccurate.

The "Gesundheit" option, German for "health," is far more common. This prompts the question: why have English-speaking North Americans adopted a German blessing for this purpose? The best answer anyone has come up with is that it was picked up from German immigrants. Some have suggested that it was learned from Yiddish-speakers, however they were more likely to respond with a variant such as "tsu gezunt."

Verbal responses to sneezes have a long and intriguing history. Aristotle was already puzzled by this phenomenon, and devoted a brief study to the question of why a sneeze is treated as a sacred event that merits more reverence than other bodily emissions like hiccups, belching or flatulence. He proposed two possible reasons: First of all, the sneeze is produced from the head, the most spiritual part of the human body, rather than the abdomen or chest. Or perhaps it is because sneezing is inextricably bound with the body's vitality. Not only does it produce a healthy benefit by easing pressures in the cerebral region, but inducing a sneeze was actually a standard medical procedure for determining whether or not a seriously damaged body was still functioning.

Ancient Jews were also accustomed to respond to sneezes —preferring the equivalent of the "Gesundheit" formula to the "Bless you." As with many practices that they shared with their non-Jewish neighbours, questions arose as to whether they might be proscribed under the Torah's prohibition of emulating "the ways of the Amorite."

The rabbinic texts are unclear with regard both to what people were saying in response to sneezes, and whether it was permissible under Jewish religious law to say those words. Some versions read the relevant passage as: "One who says *'marpe'* is following the way of the Amorite." However, most early traditions insert the word "not" into the ruling, turning it into a permission rather than a prohibition.

The Hebrew 'marpe," like its Aramaic equivalent "asuta," means "healing" or "cure" and correlates nicely with our "Gesundheit."

Quotations from the Jerusalem Talmud in medieval rabbinic works indicate that the textual tradition was still very fluid and a number of sneeze responses were preserved, including Greek phrases like "iasis" ("cure"), "zethi" ("long life"), "sos" or "soizon" ("be safe"). Similar expressions are known from Greek and Latin works, though they generally used the explicit religious formulation "may Zeus save you." Other versions of the talmudic texts give the blessing as "asuta" or the good old "le-ḥayyim."

Rabbi Menahem Meiri, though normally opposed to any practice that smacked of superstition, deemed the blessing after a sneeze unobjectionable because "anything that is said as a blessing is not a superstition, since it is said only by way of prayer.... For this reason they permitted to say 'asuta' or 'ḥayei' (life)."

Even if the rabbis were ready to absolve the sneeze-blessings from the stigma of idolatrous superstition, there remained other factors that could make them religiously problematic. Rabbi Eleazar ben Rabbi Zadok declared that one should refrain from saying "marpe" after a sneeze because of the waste of Torah study time. He reported that in the house of Rabban Gamaliel they would not say "marpe" out of concern for promoting idleness in the house of study.

Now this sounds like a very unreasonable and obsessive concern for what amounts to the loss of two syllables worth of learning time. Rashi therefore explained that the interruptions could be somewhat lengthier: while one of the students was conveying the blessing on behalf of the group, they would all have to respectfully suspend their learning so that they could pay attention and answer "Amen." This could be seriously disruptive in an educational setting that was based on memorization and oral recitation, where one could not set a bookmark or keep a finger on the page to recall where he had stopped.

Another talmudic ruling forbids responding to a sneeze while one is dining, for fear of a choking hazard. Remember that in the ancient world it was customary to eat while reclining on a couch and so one did have to be especially cautious about such matters.

Other passages take a more positive approach to sneezing, asserting that a sneeze during prayer is a favourable omen, or that it is a symptom of good health.

The most stunning explanation for why a sneeze merits a blessing is found in *Pirḳei deRabbi Eliezer*, an early medieval compendium that incorporated many obscure legends and mystical customs.

Before Jacob's death, as the patriarch was preparing to bless his grandchildren Ephraim and Manasseh, the Torah says that someone informed Joseph, "Behold, thy father is sick." The author of *Pirḳei deRabbi Eliezer* notes that this is the very first instance in scripture in which a person's death was preceded by an illness. Until that day, death would always come in a single moment. While strolling in the marketplace a person would be overcome by a sudden sneeze—and that would invariably mean that the soul was taking leave of the body through the nostrils, even as the first man had come alive when God "breathed into his nostrils the breath of life." A sneeze was thus equated with instant death.

Old Jacob pleaded before the Almighty to make some changes to the expiration process. Why not introduce an intermediate stage, when physical frailty and illness would make people aware of their approaching demise, so that they will have an opportunity to tend to arrangements for their survivors?

Jacob's wish was granted, and he was allowed a period of illness before his actual departure from the world. This was an unprecedented occurrence in human history, and it is in this connection that we are to understand the astonishment of the (unidentified) person who exclaimed to Joseph, "Behold, thy father is sick!" This was the first time since the creation that a human had not died immediately upon their first sneeze.

The *Pirḳei deRabbi Eliezer* concludes: "For this reason, whenever somebody sneezes, a person is obligated to say to them "Life!"; for that was when death in the world was transformed into light."

Sneezes may no longer be fatal, but they can spread some nasty germs. For the sake of everyone's health, please take care to cover your mouths.

Bibliography:

Askenasy, J. J. "The History of Sneezing." *Postgraduate Medical Journal* 66 (1990): 549–50.

Lieberman, Saul. *Tosefta Ki-Feshuṭah*. Vol. 3: Order Moʻed. New York: Jewish Theological Seminary of America, 1962. [Hebrew]

Preuss, Julius. *Biblical and Talmudic Medicine*. Translated by Fred Rosner. Northvale, NJ: J. Aronson, 1993.

Weiss, Shemu'el. "Ha-ʻIṭṭush be-ḤaZa"L." *Kotlenu* 13 (2010): 557–58. [Hebrew].

"Tenn. Claims of Religious Persecution Fall Apart." *Church & State*, October 2014.

First Publication

"The One that Got Away," *The Jewish Free Press*, Calgary, May 8, 2015, p. 9.

"Starting Off on the Right Foot," *The Jewish Free Press*, Calgary, August 28, 2015, p. 16.

"Who Built the Ark? Utnapishtim!" *The Jewish Free Press*, Calgary, October 9, 2015, p. 13.

"Flying out of a Rage," *The Jewish Free Press*, Calgary, October 23, 2015, p. 10.

"Symbolic Sarah," *The Jewish Free Press*, Calgary, November 6, 2015, p. 10.

"Go West, Young Jacob!" *The Jewish Free Press*, Calgary, November 20, 2015, p. 13.

"The Ultimate Space-Saver," *The Jewish Free Press*, Calgary, February 5, 2016, p. 11.

"Chariot of the God," *The Jewish Free Press*, Calgary, February 19, 2016, p. 13.

"Thrown to the Dogs," *The Jewish Free Press*, Calgary, March 18, 2016, p. 14.

"Ladies of Letters," *The Jewish Free Press*, Calgary, September 9, 2016, p. 16.

"The Messiah Takes Manhattan," *The Jewish Free Press*, Calgary, June 24, 2016, p. 13.

"Rabbis, Rationalists...and a Remedy that Roars," *The Jewish Free Press*, Calgary, October 28, 2016, p. 13.

"By the Time We Get to Phoenix," *The Jewish Free Press*, Calgary, November 11, 2016, p. 10.

"Moo-sical Mystics," *The Jewish Free Press*, Calgary, November 25, 2016, p. 13.

"Yellow Is the New Red," *The Jewish Free Press*, Calgary, March 17, 2017, p. 13.

"Fetal Positions," *The Jewish Free Press*, Calgary, May 12, 2017, p. 9.

"That Was No Lady, That Was My Allegory," *The Jewish Free Press*, Calgary, June 9, 2017, p. 9.

"Saint Gamaliel," *The Jewish Free Press*, Calgary, June 30, 2017, p. 9.

"The Poem on the Pedestal," *The Jewish Free Press*, Calgary, September 1, 2017, p. 14

"Arriving at Ararat," *The Jewish Free Press*, Calgary, October 20, 2017, p. 10.

"The Time of Our Life," *The Jewish Free Press*, Calgary, November 3, 2017, pp. 10-11.

"A Preacher's Dream and an Artist's Vision," *The Jewish Free Press*, Calgary, November 17, 2017, p. 13.

"Cagney, Kelly...and a Coin Clattering in a Keg," *The Jewish Free Press*, Calgary, February 9, 2018, p. 13.

"Wake-Up Call," *The Jewish Free Press*, Calgary, May 25, 2018, p. 13.

"What Will the Neighbours Think?" *The Jewish Free Press*, Calgary, August 24, 2018, p. 13.

"Testing the Waters," *The Jewish Free Press*, Calgary, October 5, 2018, p. 19.

"The Unkindness of Strangers," *The Jewish Free Press*, Calgary, October 19, 2018, p. 9.

"Speed Demon," *The Jewish Free Press*, Calgary, November 9, 2018, p. 13.

"It's My Party—and You'll Cry If I Want to," *The Jewish Free Press*, Calgary, December 14, 2018, p. 9.

"Dead Men Don't Sneeze," *The Jewish Free Press*, Calgary, March 22, 2019, p. 13.

www.ingramcontent.com/pod-product-compliance
Lightning Source LLC
Chambersburg PA
CBHW061636040426
42446CB00010B/1449